The Delaware General Assembly,
in granting the charter of the Library
Company of Wilmington in 1788, noted
itself "truly sensible of the advantages that
may accrue to the people of this state, by
so laudable and useful an undertaking."

So Laudable an Undertaking
The Wilmington Library, 1788-1988

Claudia L. Bushman

with an introduction by
David H. Burdash

Commissioned by the Board of Managers
of theWilmington Library
To Commemorate the 200th Anniversary of Library Service

Delaware Heritage Press
Wilmington, Delaware

SO LAUDABLE AN UNDERTAKING:
THE WILMINGTON LIBRARY, 1788-1988

A DELAWARE HERITAGE PRESS BOOK

Copyright © 1988 by Claudia L. Bushman

First Delaware Heritage Press printing, January 1989

A Delaware Heritage Commission book,
commemorating the ratification of the
Constitution of the United States by Delaware,
"The First State"

ISBN: 0-924117-00-1
Library of Congress Catalog Card Number: 88-51846

The Delaware Heritage Press
Carvel State Office Building
820 N. French Street, 4th Floor
Wilmington, Delaware

Designed by Jon R. McPheeters,
Miller Mauro Group, Inc.
Chapter Title Page Photography
by Glen R. Hampton
Typeset in Goudy Old Style
Imagesetting by am/pm Composition
Printed by Diamond Printing Co., Inc.

Contents

Preface

The Wilmington Library first came to my serious attention while I was editing two volumes of Delaware's eighteenth century legislative papers and came upon the library's request for incorporation. I was interested to learn that the library was then almost two hundred years old and to realize that service had continued in an unbroken line.

Further, three of the library's distinguished incorporators, John Dickinson, Jacob Broom, and Gunning Bedford, Jr., were Delaware representatives to the convention which wrote the United States Constitution in 1787. This fact was of particular interest while Delaware was commemorating the two hundredth anniversary of becoming "The First State" to ratify that most successful of all constitutions. As Executive Director of the Delaware Heritage Commission, which was coordinating efforts for celebration, I found the library a valuable resource. Our staff checked facts and checked out books there regularly.

This explains why I was pleased to look deeper into the library's past and to attempt to organize the considerable material into a coherent narrative. In doing so I have tried to deal with several themes. The first is the changing character of the library. The development has reflected library history in the United States, and I have tried to put Wilmington into a national context at important junctures. I have also tried to record the innovations in library work which reflect the cultural history of the period.

Libraries are pre-eminently important American institutions for educating and socializing the public, and I have touched on some of the philosophical considerations bearing on them. Libraries owe their existence to the assumption that they can and do improve society, whether that assumption is actually true or not. A major question has been whether libraries should provide patrons with the materials they want or with what they should have, in the effort to upgrade society. The libraries have largely lost this battle, currently catering to popular public wishes to keep circulation up. Whether library service is the right of citizens in a democracy and should be free to all, and which agencies—public or private—should take on the responsibility of maintaining library services, are questions still discussed. However, today's pattern of public funding with occasional private gifts is likely to continue. These are issues that I consider in this short history.

Although I have consulted many documents, the major bibliographic sources of this book have been the annual reports of the Wilmington Library. I have tried to show the library from its own position, putting its best face to the public. This is an insider view, an effort to catalog important developments in the institution's long history. A great deal of interesting material has been sacrificed to keep the narrative short and supple.

I want to acknowledge the assistance of many people in putting together these materials. Dr. John A. Munroe, Bill Frank, and Donn Devine read the manuscript and made many useful suggestions, as did Richard Abrams of the Board of Managers. Current library director David Burdash and public affairs officer Freda Campbell made library records available to me. Marjorie McNinch helped with the manuscripts at the Hagley Museum and Library. Drs. Constance Cooper and Barbara Benson and Ellen Peterson at the Historical Society of Delaware provided invaluable assistance. Jean Bingham, Lynda Cook, and Marguerite Sheridan made excellent suggestions as well as assisting in compiling material. Some of the many people who talked to me about the library and their experience with it are acknowledged in the bibliography.

The Wilmington Library is a unique cultural presence in the City, open, as libraries are fond of saying, to all comers. Inner city residents and suburbanites who work in the City count on the rich resources which are available without appointment and without fee. Even those who seldom visit the library regard its presence as comforting and ennobling.

Claudia L. Bushman
1988

Introduction

Upon the occasion of celebrating two hundred years of uninterrupted service to residents of Wilmington and New Castle County, the Wilmington Library sincerely appreciates the publication of *So Laudable An Undertaking: The Wilmington Library, 1788 to 1988,* by Dr. Claudia L. Bushman, historian, lecturer, author, and dear friend of the Library.

Writing a history of an institution is, at the very least, a complex undertaking. The gathering of often-times confusing and sometimes contradictory information, the assignment of relevance to seemingly insignificant episodes which cumulate to cause important events, and the final explanation of historical, social and cultural experiences within an institution require the curiosity of an information specialist, the determination of a sleuth, and the creativity of an exciting storyteller.

Dr. Bushman has combined all of these skills with patience, good humor, and a love of.libraries to provide a stimulating account of the evolution of the Wilmington Library. Her research has revealed much information regarding the early ordeals in establishing and maintaining the Library and has led her to conclusions objectively stated and to results clearly defined. The interweaving and knitting together of the descriptions of important milestones in the development of the early library, interconnected by smooth transitions of interesting socio-economic explanations for the direction of current library services are provided by a flowing narrative style warmly welcomed by readers of history.

Photographs of the services and personalities of those who impacted on the long and distinguished history of the Library, as well as representations of architectural features of the current central library also flow throughout the volume adding a vital pictorial account of the institution's growth. Those of us who have become attached to the beauty of the building on Rodney Square truly appreciate the work of the photographers from the past and present who have contributed to the Library's archival materials.

During the two hundred years of public service, the Board of Managers and staff of the Library have obviously played important roles in the development of the institution. In her history, Dr. Bushman often refers to the extraordinary contributions of the Managers who personally guaranteed the continuation of service during difficult financial periods. She also describes the dedication of the staff who serve the public daily or support public services from behind the scenes. Because of their sensitivity to public demands and their sense of responsibility for excellence in service, Managers and Staff are commended and celebrated by Dr. Bushman's vivid narrative.

As the Library begins its third century of service, the staff and Board of Managers of the Library find particular interest in Dr. Bushman's reminder that the Library, as we know it today, is a product of their hard work and dedication, as well as the generous support of interested and loyal library patrons. The common thread which links the Library's present to its illustrious past is the public/private partnership which created the Library and so generously supports it today. For that support we will be eternally grateful.

David H. Burdash
Director
The Wilmington Library

Illustrations

Pictures are in the collections of the Wilmington Library unless otherwise noted. Many were copied by Wade Lawrence for a 200th anniversary exhibition on the history of the library. The pictures which begin each chapter are details from the bas relief of the facade or the interior frieze of the library building at 10th and Market Streets.

So Laudable An Undertaking
The Wilmington Library, 1788-1988

ONE

The Shadowy Beginnings, 1754 to 1763

HE WILMINGTON LIBRARY, THE GRAND OLD LADY OF THE CITY'S CULTURAL INSTITUTIONS, HAS MOVED STEADILY NORTHWARD ON MARKET STREET IN HER 200 YEARS OF EXISTENCE. THE LIBRARY, CHARTERED IN 1788, THE YEAR AFTER DELAWAREANS DISTINGUISHED THEMSELVES BY VOTING FIRST AND UNANIMOUSLY TO RATIFY THE UNITED STATES Constitution, has witnessed many changes in this little city. Her own developments reflect the changing world around her. Established as a small elite Quaker effort to share books, the library is now the bastion of information and high and low culture for all, serving the people of the State as well as those of the County and the City.

Further, the Wilmington Library is a microcosm of library development over the years. The story combines the benefits of generous and far sighted private philanthropy, the contributions of the masses, and the growing responsibility of the government. Changes here reflect steadily increasing library professionalism, and the difficulties of funding a complex operation which is expected to be free to the public. All these factors, contributions, and influences have played parts in the first two centuries of the library which has brought information, education, and entertainment to many generations of Delawareans.

Although the ancient world possessed notable libraries, and the church and universities collected books to further their own ends, the beginnings of the library system as we know it emerged in the 18th century when groups organized to share books. Wilmington's library was respectably early. That it still exists after 200 years, when all but a few comparable early institutions have succumbed, illustrates the tenacity and adaptability of its founders and their successors.

A rudimentary Wilmington library apparently began in 1754, long before the official charter in 1788, although the history of this small institution is largely unrecorded. The only evidence of this early library, so far discovered, is a receipt signed by D. Benjamin Ferris, for his father, the treasurer, crediting Joseph Tatnall for paying his library dues. The receipt documents the 9th Annual Payment of library dues of five shillings, dated November 12, 1763, and is stamped, "Wilming-

1. Wilmington, 1790, at the time the library was organized. Courtesy, Historical Society of Delaware.

ton Library, 1754."[1] This is good evidence that the library lasted at least nine years.

A small circulation library in the Quaker community could well have been in regular operation. That libraries existed in small colonial towns is not unusual. Scores of similar libraries were springing up along the Atlantic seaboard in the mid-eighteenth century.

A letter supporting the existence of an early library and its short

life was sent to the Wilmington Borough Council, when the Library Association petitioned in 1816 to use Town Hall.

The inhabitants established a Public Library (under favor of the Police who granted the Company their Council Chamber) that had arrived to a State of Considerable respectability, when the events of the War of the American Revolution put this town into the possession of the British Army, at which time the Library was destroyed or carried off by the officers of that army.[2]

2. Joseph Tatnall, an early subscriber of the Wilmington Library. Courtesy, Historical Society of Delaware.

This account may well be true, but the facts are vague, and the account itself was written almost fifty years after services were disrupted by the disappearance of the books. In any case, very little is known of the first library in Wilmington.

America has always retained an ancient and primitive homage for books. Early inventories of Delawareans of moderate wealth generally include a few books,[3] and the library movement reflects an eagerness to read more than those few personal books by pooling volumes with friends. Faith in education has been an American assumption since the nation was founded. Education would enable a man to read the Bible for himself and to become, regardless of birth or position, a worthy citizen. Faith in the perfectability of man, a basic tenet of the Enlightenment, is reflected in the thought of such

3. The receipt issued to Joseph Tatnall by D. Benjamin
Ferris, the son of the treasurer of Wilmington Library,
Nov. 12, 1763.

founding fathers as Jefferson and Franklin. Free public schooling was
an early, if unrealized, goal, and the library has taken the position next
to the school as the fount of available knowledge.

Benjamin Franklin is generally credited with establishing the
earliest American subscription library in Philadelphia in 1731. After
a first informal library where members of his young men's club, the
Junto, brought their books to the club room for reference, Franklin
followed a pattern currently used in England and Scotland. He drew
up proposals and had the organization chartered for fifty years. The
Library Company of Philadelphia enlisted fifty members, then one
hundred, who initially paid forty shillings each and ten shillings
annual dues. The Philadelphia group ordered books from England
and set up the library, first in the house of a member, and later the
State House and the Carpenters' Hall.

With characteristic modesty, Franklin credited the fast growing
library with improving the general conversation of the Americans,
making the "common tradesmen and farmers as intelligent as most
gentlemen from other countries," and even contributing to the
energy the American patriots displayed in defending their country.[4]
Such rhetoric exemplifies the American belief in the power of
learning.

Franklin's institution was really a joint stock company in which
each member of the company owned one or more shares. These shares
could be bought and sold like any others. This "proprietary" form of

the social library became the major model. Another model, the athenaeum, emphasized the availability of scholarly newspapers and magazines as well as cultural and recreational activities. The Boston Athenaeum founded in 1807 remains a successful example.

The Library Company of Philadelphia model was adopted by other states which established subscription libraries. Connecticut had four before 1740.[5] Many were shortlived, succumbing to the limited availability of voluntary financial support. In bad times, library membership was a luxury easily sacrificed. Wilmington's earliest library fell victim in this way.

TWO

The Library Company of Wilmington, 1788-1859

N DECEMBER 12, 1787, THE *DELAWARE GAZETTE* RAN A NO-
TICE INVITING "ALL PERSONS WHO INCLINED TO JOIN THE NEW LIBRARY TO
MEET AT THE TOWN HALL" ON DECEMBER 15. OF THE GROUP THAT GATH-
ERED THAT NIGHT, FIVE MEN, CHARLES H. WHARTON, NICHOLAS WAY,
JACOB BROOM, THOMAS LEA, AND JAMES LEA, JR., WERE APPOINTED A
committee "to prepare a sett of Articles, likewise a Catalogue of such
Books as they may think suitable," and report back. The Wilmington
library began its second life in 1788, a life which has continued
uninterrupted, in various forms, since that meeting in the Town Hall
over the Second Street Market House.

At that time Wilmington was a thriving town with a population
of 2,000. Visitors commented on the straight streets, the market
house, and the academy on a hill. Several hundred houses, many of
them of brick, housed an industrious populace.[1]

The organizers of the infant library prepared Articles of Association which were adopted on January 9, 1788. Jacob Broom was elected
treasurer. Other directors included Patrick Murdock; William Poole;
William Hemphill; John Hayes; James Lea, Jr.; Peter Brynberg; James
Robinson, Jr.; Joseph Warner; and John Ferris. "Being willing and
desirous to promote Knowledge of good Literature," they "whose
Names [were] hereunto subscribed and seals affixed," signed their
names and drew in little seal-like designs.

They covenanted to form a joint stock company for the purpose
of purchasing books to establish a library. They agreed to pay the
treasurer "forty shillings in gold or silver coin lawful money of the
Delaware State, and seven shillings & six pence each Year afterwards,
so long as a Majority of the Company shall Judge it necessary." These
fees were similar to those charged by the Library Company of

4. Preamble of the Articles of Association of the Library Company of Wilmington, dated January 9, 1788.

Philadelphia. The new group was busy from December through April, meeting every two weeks or so, preparing to open the library. Committee members assembled a list of desired books which was sent to Philadelphia to be priced, and when the first report came back at about £100, they ordered the books bought. Several of the group went out to solicit subscriptions and signed up their friends.

The members prepared a constitution for the Library Company of Wilmington with a seal saying "A Book in Hand" and "Wilmington Library 1788" around it. The annual election of a treasurer and director and the appointment of a librarian on the first Monday in September were called for.

On March 27, the Library Company hired Isaac Starr, Jr. to be librarian for a year. Starr was sufficiently devoted to the cause to remain as a member of the board for forty years. His salary as librarian was £3, and his instructions were to attend the library from 3-5 on Saturday from October 1 to March 1 and from 5-7 the rest of the year. He was to lend a folio or quarto for six weeks, an octavo for four weeks, and four pamphlets for three weeks, after the members signed promisory notes for twice the cost of each book. Non-members could

5. The engraving seal of the Wilmington Library, dated 1788, shows evidence of having been changed from the earlier date of 1754.

borrow these books, according to the librarian's instructions, for fees varying from four to eight pence per week per volume depending on size. Frederick Craig, a printer like Brynberg, bound volumes as needed. The library first opened its doors on April 4, 1788.[2]

The "Members of the Library Company of Wilmington" petitioned the General Assembly for incorporation. The charter was granted on June 11, 1788.

The incorporators of the library, all the paid-up members by June of 1788, were an impressive group, headed by John Dickinson, the "penman of the Revolution," and included Thomas May; Charles H.

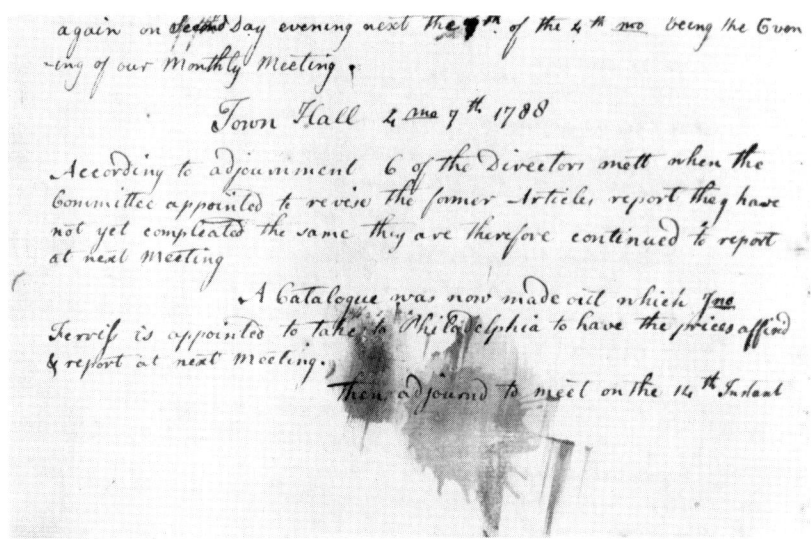

6. Minutes of the Library Company of Wilmington, April 7, 1788.

Wharton; Jacob Broom; Joseph Warner; John Ferris; John Hayes; William Poole; James Robinson, Jr.; Isaac Hendrickson, Jr.; John Thelwell; James Brobson; Henry Paschall; Israel Brown; Samuel Byrnes; Thomas Robinson; William Robinson; Patrick Murdoch; John Martin; Frederick Craig; John Clark; Francis Way; Henry Reynolds; Ebenezer A. Smith; Joshua Jackson; Sarah Frisby; Philip Bonsall; William Sharply, Jr.; William Corbitt; Daniel J. Adams; Joseph Capelle; John McKinly; Gunning Bedford, Jr.; John Rumsey; Joseph Summerl; Joseph Shipley; James Delaplain; Jehu Hollingsworth, Jr.; Thomas Lea; and Isaac Starr. They noted that they had "at a considerable expence, purchased a large and valuable collection of useful books" to form a library in Wilmington, "for the advancement of knowledge and literature." Incorporation would enable them to receive and hold donations and bequests. The General Assembly, in granting the charter noted itself "truly sensible of the advantages that may accrue to the people of this state, by so laudable and useful an undertaking."[3]

When librarian Starr's term was over, Stephen Hayes served briefly and Robert Coram was appointed on December 10, 1789 at a salary of £4 s10. Coram was also influential in the organization of the

New Castle Library Company in 1811.[4] The directors voted on April 5, 1790 to move the books to Robert Coram's school house on High Street, a convenient site for the librarian and members. Even in the eighteenth century when books were rare and expensive, they got lost. The directors had previously decided that the librarian was responsible for all the books loaned out, and after John Webster became the next librarian on December 11, 1790, for $12 a year, the managers were at some pains to "demand" the outstanding books from Coram who slowly located and returned the volumes. Four years later, the directors were still trying to settle Coram's account.[5]

The minute book of 1787-1818 of the library dealt mostly with delinquent dues payers, books to be purchased, and the election of directors. Many of the directors were re-elected year after year. Only once is there a suggestion of outreach to the community when on February 5, 1801 the "directors took into consideration the great probability that a number of the Inhabitants of this Borough might join the Company if applied to" and agreed to solicit their friends; a few new members were welcomed. Some of these new members offered books in lieu of paying dues.

Others left the association. Those with overdue fees were required to pay up or to pay a fee for each borrowed book. Many early members are crossed off the lists, probably indicating that they had moved or sold their shares. When Sarah Frisby, the sole female charter member, was confronted with the news that her membership payments were in arrears, she simply gave up the project and relinquished all rights to the library.

On December 2, 1793, when Peter Brynberg proposed Edward Hewes to be the new librarian, and Hewes agreed to serve for a fee of $14 a year, which included furnishing a suitable room to serve as library, he also needed to join the association. The $6.33 membership charge was deducted from his salary, leaving only a small net profit. This transaction suggests that no present member was interested in serving as librarian, and that recruiting took place outside of the group. Hewes also joined the Board and served as secretary. In order to attract librarians, the compensation was steadily raised. In 1796, the librarian's fee was raised to $20 because of the increased books and services involved. In 1803, he was paid $32, and $45 in 1809. By 1811, the salary was up to $50.

We whose Names are hereunto subscribed and seals affixed, being willing and desirous to promote Knowledge & good Literature, do hereby covenant and agree, each one for himself, to & with each other, to form a Joint stock for the purpose of purchasing a Collection of Books to compose a Library in the Borough of Wilmington, to be called the Wilmington Library, that each one of us will pay into the Hands of a Treasurer hereafter to be Named or his Successor the sum of forty shillings in Gold or Silver coin lawful money of the Delaware State, and seven shillings & six pence each Year afterwards, so long as a Majority of the Company shall Judge it necessary & that we who shall have subscribed or so

7. Constitution of the Library Company of Wilmington, Jan 5, 1788.

The Library Company of Wilmington grew both by membership and by aggregation. In 1803, the Amicable Society apparently closed down. The unknown organization had a balance of funds of eight and a half dollars which came to the library. In 1805 John Dickinson donated five shares of stock in the Spring Water Company of Wilmington to the library.[6]

On March 23, 1816, the library moved to a small room on the southwest corner, second floor, of Town Hall.[7] That year a single share of stock cost six dollars, which was collected by Peter Brynberg, then the library treasurer as well as a printer and bookseller. The library remained in Town Hall until 1851 when it was moved to the rooms of the Athenaeum Company in the market house at Fourth and Market Streets.

In 1818 the longtime custom of lending books for a fee to people who were not members of the library was discontinued. The directors particularly objected to non-members' checking out books on share-holders' cards without posting notes for the books' value. The reason

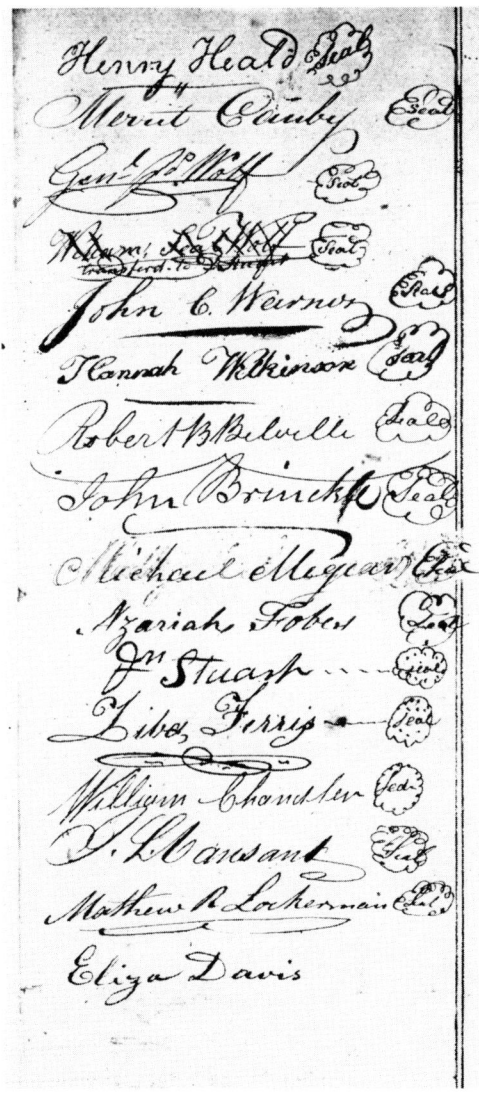

8. Partial list of signatures of the original directors of the Wilmington Library with the individual "seal" of each individual.

given was that "it placed Shareholders at a disadvantage." Along with this regressive move toward elitism, the cost of shares was advanced to ten dollars to make up for any lost revenue. The increased price was not a success and in 1828 the board decided to divide forfeited shares and charge five dollars for each half. This move increased the number of shareholders and the funds available.[8] With hindsight it is clear that a broader membership at a lesser price would have benefitted the institution, but this direction was not followed until much later.

The most colorful incident recorded in the early minute book took place in 1809 in connection with a new book, *Address to the Congress of the United States* by C. B. Brown of Philadelphia.[9] The book contained offensive statements "incompatible with truth, tending to subvert all distinction between right and wrong, virtue and vice." The investigating committee reported the complaint against the book well founded because the author had contended that England had as much right to exclude the United States from navigating the ocean as the States did to navigate it. This "subverting all known and established principles of Justice & equity by Substituting power for right" persuaded the committee "to declare their Abhorrence of Such detestable principles," and as a suitable fate, they recommended that the book "be burned by the hands of the librar-

9. Stock certificate for the Library Company of Wilmington, 1834.

ian," a drastic prescription which was, in fact, carried out.[10] The Quaker merchants who made up the bulk of library members were understandably sensitive about their rights to carry their milled flour on the high seas, but this censorship seems remarkably stern.

Delawareans lived on the edge of the cultural center in Philadelphia, closely tied to that capitol by their political designation as the Three Lower Counties, by the Quaker connection, and by the Delaware River which made frequent travel to Philadelphia relatively convenient. Several Delawareans were members of Philadelphia's American Philosophical Society, even as they began intellectual groups of their own.

Learned groups organized in Wilmington included the related Delaware Philosophical Society, which studied natural philosophy;

the Lyceum; the Medical Society of Delaware; and the Society for the Suppression of Vice and Immorality. These fledgling groups were animated by an idealistic vision of a society of learned companions. In practical terms, they had their difficulties, and many had short lives. The papers of the Medical Society record complaints that attendance was poor and that current dues were badly needed to pay debts. The Lyceum debates became too personal with political backbiting.

The Philosophical Society disbanded. The agricultural societies repeatedly failed to attract broad membership. The Library Company complained of a lack of public interest, and in 1817 was forced to

10. Wilmington's Old Town Hall, constructed in 1798, is shown here in 1860. Courtesy, Historical Society of Delaware.

borrow funds from the Society of Friends to keep afloat; the money was not repaid until 1853. Annual memberships for $2 were instituted to keep the organization alive. The only two eighteenth-century learned societies in Wilmington which remain with us today are the Library and the Medical Society of Delaware, which survived by adapting to meet changing times.[11]

Reading materials burgeoned during the last half of the 18th century. By 1762 the American colonies had fifty-one weekly newspapers and twelve American magazines, which were widely read.[12] Few people could own all the books they wanted, and alternatives to ownership began to develop. Coffeehouses in the big cities, similar to those in London, ordered all the newspapers and served as reading rooms. Hostelries and livery stables housed post offices and had newspapers to read and books to buy.[13]

After the Revolution more books were printed locally.[14] The number of newspapers increased rapidly. New England numbered 51 social libraries like Wilmington's before 1780 and 325 before the end of the century.[15]

The Library Company of Wilmington, a subscription library, where voluntary membership was open to individuals who contributed money to buy books for common use and who paid an annual fee for the privilege of borrowing the books, was not to be confused with any of the commercially operated circulating libraries. Circulating libraries, very popular during this period in England and the United States, provided reading materials which could be rented for use. These business operations were often conducted with perfumery, haberdashery, or stationery shops; the subscription libraries were voluntary and private. The reading tastes of subscription libraries were largely belles-lettres and political science. The circulating libraries moved more toward novels.[16]

Circulating libraries flourished in England in the eighteenth century, particularly in the watering places such as Bath. The libraries reflected a major change in public reading patterns as large groups were able to read for the first time, and many individuals were learning to read for pleasure. Fashionable ladies consumed novels at a great rate, as did their maids.[17] The libraries carried serious works besides novels and were frequented by people of substance, but their public image was of pandering to the frivolous needs of leisured women, and the libraries were ridiculed and scorned in the satires of the day.

The United States also had circulating libraries of the English style. William Rind of Annapolis seems to have established the first, which failed in 1762. At least eleven circulating libraries were in operation in six American cities in the fourteen years prior to the Revolution. Notable was the "New Circulating Library" of Lewis Nicola in Philadelphia at Race and Vine Streets. Nicola began with three hundred or so books of history, fiction, poetry, plays, and travel, and increased the number steadily until by 1771 he had more than one thousand.[18] Many of these American circulating libraries were operated in connection with booksellers, though Mary Sprague and Kezia Butler of Boston ran theirs with two separate millinery shops.[19] Nicola shared his premises with Ellenor Fitzgerald, a milliner, indicating the largely female nature of his clientele. Caritat's Circulating Library in New York City, opened in 1797, had over 5,000 volumes in its catalog by 1804. Twenty percent were fiction. The Erie Canal even had a "Book Boat" which would tie up at the towns from Albany to Buffalo and rent out books.[20]

By contrast, an early catalog of the books in the Library Company of Wilmington, undated, but probably from about 1800 according to the publication dates of some of its books, is very serious indeed. A count of the books yields about 336 titles, and because some have several parts, 755 volumes. Not all can be categorized easily, but history (52, 15%) and travel and geography (59, 18%) top the list, with 32 volumes of biography and letters, 17 of divinity, 27 which might be political science, philosophy, and law, 21 of science and 11 of agriculture. Among the books still well known are the poetic works of Pope, Milton, Goldsmith, and Homer, though Shakespeare is absent. The scientific works of Priestly, Benjamin Rush, and Count Rumford are represented. The works of John Dickinson and local inventor Oliver Evans with his *The Young Mill-wright and Millers' Guide* represent local authors. Several titles deal specifically with women, including the unknown *Accomplished Woman, Letters on the Female Mind*, the *Ladies Library* in two volumes, and Mary Wortly Montague's *Rights of Women*. Several others indicate opposition to slavery, a major tenet of Quaker thought. Although novels were the staples of the circulating library, only Defoe's *Robinson Crusoe* is recognizable as one here, along with *Observation on Novel Reading*, which promises to be critical of the habit. The Library Company of Wilmington had a very high minded collection.[21] The Charitable Library of Concord, Massachusetts, which held a mere 76 volumes in the 1790s,[22] took a similar stand. If the young women wanted novels, which were readily available, they would have to purchase them themselves.[23]

Benjamin Franklin's Library Company of Philadelphia reflected similar tastes. A breakdown of the 375 titles listed in the 1741 catalogue can be roughly divided as follows: history, 114 (30%); social sciences, 28; arts, 13; linguistics, 10; and general 5. Most were in English and dealt with history and science. An analysis of the holdings of thirteen other social libraries in New England between 1760 and 1841 reveals a similar preponderance of books about theology, history, biography, and travel, with somewhat more novels.[24] By comparison, an analysis of the Harvard College library holdings in 1735, indicates that that collection was two thirds theological.[25]

The fiction in the New England social libraries ranged from five to twenty percent between 1785 and 1841, but readers probably selected a much larger percentage of fiction than that. Thomas Jefferson was against novel reading, calling the whole genre a "mass of trash," but the steady rise in the American publication of novels shows a population hungry for light reading and eager to purchase it.[26]

Circulating libraries of various kinds continued in operation until almost the present time, eventually done in by television and video rental outfits. Circulating libraries with books for hire provide a significant chapter in the history of libraries. Because the owners were working for profits, they were quick to innovate while association libraries were conservative. These commercial librarians tried new services which were often later adopted by association and free libraries and which became the standard style. They were willing to serve women and in fact were often run by women in places frequented by women. They provided popular books, fiction and belles-lettres. They were open long hours from the beginning, in connection with other services and provided reading rooms, or at least chairs, while other libraries could only be open a few hours a week. Home delivery was sometimes offered, and even branch outlets. Public libraries now do all these things, even offering new books and reserved books for fees in many circumstances.

Circulating libraries could never overcome their greatest disadvantages, that they could command no prestige and respectability due to their non-exclusive nature and finally, that they received no tax support while their competitors did.[27] Yet their history is important in the development of the libraries we know today.

THREE

The
Wilmington Institute,
1859-1894

N 1849, THE ROOM IN THE TOWN HALL WHERE THE LIBRARY WAS HOUSED WAS NEEDED FOR OTHER ACTIVITIES. THE LIBRARY WAS RELOCATED BRIEFLY IN THE WILSON BUILDING, AT THE CORNER OF FIFTH AND MARKET STREETS, BEFORE ARRANGEMENTS WERE MADE WITH THE ATHENAEUM COMPANY TO USE THEIR BUILDING OVER THE FOURTH STREET Market House. Five members of the Library Company bought shares in the Athenaeum's joint-stock building, taking it over for the Library which paid interest to the investors. The Library moved to the site in 1851.[1] In these new quarters the library established extended hours of 7-10 every evening.

The Library continued to grow by assimilation, gathering in organizations which had flowered and gone to seed. In 1846 the Young Men's Library and Debating Society, afterwards the Franklin Lyceum, united with the Library Company. This association, founded in 1834, had once possessed over 800 books and four hundred dollars worth of "philosophical apparatus," now sadly diminished. Each member of the Lyceum was issued a share in the Library Company.[2]

In the great age of self-improvement in the United States, Wilmington spawned a number of these societies of mutual improvement. The Athenaeum sponsored speeches. The Debating Society explored the issues of the day. The Juvenile Literary Society encouraged a taste for books.[3] Most societies eventually merged with the library. The library, rather than providing books for a small learned group, began to broaden its membership.

In 1853, the Botanical and Horticultural Societies deposited their books there. The Delaware Academy of Natural Sciences granted the library the interest of a $500 fund to purchase scientific books.

Ðo Ãei Ãeiki Coke Ãai Ãebera.

THUG

The Vomitories of the Aballaboozabanganorribonean
Mokuna will be patefacted this evening at 7¼
o'clock.

Grapheus.

Saturday, 185

11. Admission ticket for Aballaboozabanganorribonean
Mokuna, 1850-1855.

The Young Men's Association for Mutual Improvement, another
learned group, succeeded a literary society dating from 1847 which
was known by the dashing name of the Aballiboozabanganorribonean Mokuna. This group of wags met in Mokuna Hall at East
Sixth Street in Wilmington. The meaning of their colorful name is
lost in obscurity, though it may refer to dancing, drinking, and noise.
The Aballiboozabanganorribonean Mokuna's stock and membership
were bought up by The Young Men's Association, which had organized on September 22, 1855 and incorporated February 10, 1857. This
respectably named organization met on Third Street, west of Market
Street, and the secretary recorded that "It was truly gratifying to the
Executive Committee to witness so large a display of intelligence
assembled." The group instituted a reading room, with a wide variety
of newspapers and magazines, and a popular course of lectures, open
to the public and free to members. "Everything undertaken by the
Association has succeeded beyond the expectations of the most
sanguine," commented the scribe.[4]

Under the direction of President T. Clarkson Taylor, the group
moved to form a stock company, establish a scientific department,
and make preliminary arrangements to erect a hall. Membership,
after approval by the group, was available for one dollar admission and
three dollars a year, and stood at 350 members.

In 1856 the Library Company and the Young Men's Association
for Mutual Improvement considered a serious merger, whenever the

26

latter organization should acquire property worth $5,000. In the meantime, the Young Men would have the use of the library for one year for a total cost of $150.[5]

When the agreement expired, without merger, and the library cut off the reading privileges of the Young Men, the latter group moved to begin another library, quickly raising $2,160.[6] The Wilmington Library then once again entered into negotiations for merger, and union was achieved. The Young Men's Association was to pay $1000 and to erect a building of the same size at the rear of that occupied by the library. Most of the 4,500 books came from the library, but most of the 450 members came from the Young Men's group. The joint association elected J. T. Heald, William S. Hilles, George W. Bush, John P. McLoud, Edward T. Taylor, and William H. Billany as the first executive committee, with successors to be elected annually.[7]

The joint group was incorporated under the name The Wilmington Institute by the Delaware General Assembly on January 27, 1859, for the purpose of "establishing and maintaining a Library, Reading Room, Literary and Scientific Lectures, Debates, and other means for promoting social, moral and intellectual advancement."[8]

Early presidents stated explicitly their hope that the lectures, books, and reading rooms would help boys who had left school, and maybe home as well, at an early age, to learn their trades and a love of reading, safe from the temptations of the street.[9]

Libraries to serve mechanics and mercantile interests were forming around the country at this time.[10] The first mechanics' libraries had appeared in Glasgow (1760) and Birmingham

12. Title page of the Constitution of the Young Men's Association for Mutual Improvement, 1855.

PREAMBLE.

We the undersigned feeling that our combined and concentrated efforts, in generally diffusing the means of information would, in the extension of like benefits to all conduce to the improvement of each, have associated ourselves together for the establishing and maintaining of a Reading Room, Library, Literary and Scientific Lectures, Debates, and other means of mutual improvement, and do adopt the following for our

Constitution.

Chapter 1st.
Of Members.

Article 1st. This Association shall be known as "The Young Men's Association for Mutual Improvement" of the City of Wilmington.

Article 2nd. Any person between the ages of fifteen and forty five, may if approved by the Executive Committee, become a regular member by paying an initiation fee of One Dollar and the further sum of One Dollar and fifty cents

13. Preamble to the Constitution of the Young Men's Association for Mutual Improvement, 1855.

(1795) where industrialization was rapidly expanding the economic lower middle class. Workingmen's lectures and a reading room were offered for one penny a week. By the early 1820s mechanics' institutes and libraries had been organized in Boston, Portland, Philadelphia, and New York to socialize workers into industry, promote orderly and virtuous habits, spread knowledge, and turn rural louts and uneducated boys into good citizens and productive workers and managers. These humanitarian aims were coupled with the practical enhancement of skills and efforts to help the young grow and develop.[11] These libraries were often the beneficence of captains of industry, many of whom remembered patrons who had helped them up the ladder of learning.

One such princely institution was erected in the City of Baltimore which received $1,400,000 in 1851 from George Peabody, a prosperous businessman operating in London. Peabody's plan is instructive of the sort of cultural activities then deemed suitable. The institute should teach political and religious harmony and toleration by organizing an extensive library, well furnished in every department but medicine and law, providing lectures by accomplished scholars and men of science, and establishing an academy of music and a gallery of fine arts.[12]

The paternalism of these institutions was only slightly polluted by self-interest, and workers genuinely appreciated the opportunities available at these institutions. In many ways the founders of these industrial institutes showed the same faith in scientific knowledge and education as the eighteenth century library organizers.[13]

This movement was well underway before Wilmington's Institute was organized in the 1850s. Ambitious and far reaching, the Wilmington officers decided to create a large building to house their activities. Later leaders marveled at their audacity. In 1888, Isaac T.

14. The John Dickinson House, Market Street at 8th Street, which was replaced by the Wilmington Institute building. Photo, about 1859, by H. S. Garrett, Wilmington. Courtesy of the Historical Society of Delaware.

Johnson, president of the Institute, said, "When we consider the size of Wilmington in 1860 and the condition of the country at that time we cannot but admire the enterprise and courage of those who undertook to raise funds to erect the building."[14]

The Wilmington Institute sold the property over the Fourth Street Market House, which they had purchased from the Athenaeum Company, to the city authorities for two thousand dollars[15] and purchased a site for a permanent home at Eighth and Market Streets from Mrs. John P. Gilles for thirteen thousand dollars. The land and the grand house on it, had been owned by John Dickinson, one of the first incorporators of the library, and had been sold twice before. The lot extended from Market to Shipley Streets, the house facing Kent Street, now Eighth Street, and was enclosed by a high brick wall. Besides the elegant house, the lot was elevated, "commanding an extensive view of the surrounding country, and for health and convenience [it was] excelled by none."[16]

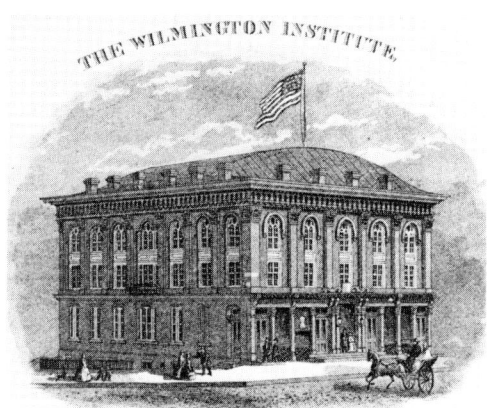

15. The Wilmington Institute building from a letterhead engraving, about 1864. Engraved by M. H. Trumble, Philadelphia.

The President and Treasurer were authorized to borrow twenty thousand dollars to complete the new building which was reported to cost $40,823.14. Under this mortgage, the officers issued forty bonds, each for five hundred dollars, under the corporate seal of the Wilmington Institute. Dated 1861, the bonds paid six per cent a year, and the interest was paid semi-annually. Four bonds came due each year and were retired.[17]

The cornerstone was laid June 24, 1860, and the auditorium, or Hall of the new building, was inaugurated on January 30, 1861, with an address by Daniel M. Bates, a historical sketch of the association by the Rev. G. F. Wiswell, and music by the Amateur Glee Club."[18]

16. The Wilmington Institute Free Library Building, looking north from 8th Street, Wilmington, 1861. From a postcard in the collection of the Wilmington Library.

At no time has the actual condition of the Institute been as favorable, at no time have its capabilities and prospects of accomplishing the noble objects, been as flattering as now," the president reported. Membership was up by 100 to 666.[19]

The Wilmington Institute had erected the finest building in the city, and the Hall, which could seat eight hundred, was the only theatre in town. The Hall and the Reading Room of the library were on the second floor, reachable from the back side of the building.[20] The large and small lecture halls, as well as the stairway and the committee room, were rented to groups for their events. On the ground floor were a number of small shops which were leased to local businessmen at quarterly fees, as were several upstairs offices. The reading room of the library, which opened March 11, 1861, was to be available from 7 am to 10 pm, a very long day.

As the officers faced the first year in the new building, they estimated their annual expenses and figured that they should gross about $2,500 from renting their halls, stores, and offices, and about $1,800 from members' initiation fees and dues. They estimated operating expenses at under $1,000. The big expenses were $2,050 in interest on their debt and $500 to buy each bond as it fell due. They figured $300 for books, $180 for newspapers and magazines, $50 for laboratory equipment for their science projects, and $100 to print circulars for their lecture series. They expected that the lectures themselves would be self-supporting, a supposition which was not born out.[21]

Each of the hard-working Standing Committees of the Institute reported weekly on the work assigned. The Library Committee listed the books ordered and received; the Rooms and Fixtures Committee rented out the spaces and arranged for manpower and maintenance. The Ways and Means Committee devoted itself to enlisting new membership and collecting dues. The Lecture Committee corresponded with potential lecturers, negotiated fees, and scheduled such notable speakers as Edward Everett, Horace Greeley, Henry Ward Beecher, Frederick Douglass, Wendell Phillips, and Anna Dickinson. The Printing Committee prepared circulars and certificates. The Debating Committee scheduled verbal contests which waxed and waned in popularity. The Periodicals and Newspapers Committee ordered about seventy-five daily, weekly, monthly, and quarterly serials for the reference room, and recommended subscriptions. The Donations Committee acknowledged the books and other items which were given to the Institute.

The Library Committee continued to buy important and useful books, and even threw out a few. On June 26, 1866, the committee requested that the library withdraw from circulation *Moll Flanders* and the *History of the Devil* and destroy them. *Mosley and His Men* was also withdrawn. Someone objected to the purchase of Polland's *Life of Jefferson Davis*. *Gates Wide Open* was removed as unsuitable.[22]

In 1864 the Archives Committee moved to organize a department to encourage historical inquiry and research and to diffuse historical information—natural and civil, ancient and modern—within the state. This new department was to be called the Historical Society of the Wilmington Institute.[23] The historical group set up a cabinet of curiosities for rare and interesting donations such as preserved birds, the sword of a swordfish, and confederate money.

William S. Hilles, the president of the Institute noted that:

The time is come when every trace and relic of the original settlers of the banks of the Delaware, and of colonial and revolutionary times, ought to be jealously preserved. The historian of future times will have reason to reflect upon our want of foresight if we take no pains to prevent these things from being squandered and wasted in the shifting and uncertain hands of families and individuals.[24]

The committee prepared and distributed a circular inviting interested parties to meet at the Institute "to unite in perfecting a plan to secure the better illustration of the history of Delaware." However, at the meeting, the group decided that the Wilmington Institute, a city unit, was too restrictive a sponsor for a historical group with interests encompassing the whole state. The Historical Society of Delaware, an independent agency, was organized on that occasion and dates its beginning on May 31, 1864.[25]

The Institute opened its doors to learned societies such as the Medical Society of the State of Delaware which could rent its facilities and to uplifting programs of all kinds. The Hall rented for $25 an evening, $20 for a lecture, $35 for an evening political event, and $10 for an afternoon entertainment. An approved group could rent the Hall for a week for $120.

The application of Sarah J. Carpenter to use the scientific lecture room to deliver lectures on electropathy and private lectures on the diseases of women was approved. The Ladies' Aid Society of Grace Church was allowed to erect a fountain in the Hall for their festival, and the Horticultural Society set up a fountain for their exhibition as well.

The Board was careful about the uses to which the Hall would be put. Dancing was generally banned. The Excelsior Brass Band was not allowed to use the Hall for a ball. Board members rejected the request of the "Diamond State Guards" to hold a party. They refused to rent the basement room for a "Billiard Saloon." [27]

Occasionally they opened their doors too far. The Rooms and Fixtures Committee reported that the librarian had, "under the impression that there was nothing improper in it, engaged the Hall to an agent of the party known as the "Davenport Boys" who give public exhibitions styled Spiritual Manifestations... It having since appeared to the committee that these exhibitions are of an immoral character and also tend to disorder the com.[munity] [they] desire to annul the engagement of the hall therefor." The board of directors gave the "Davenport Boys" back their $5 deposit, and also had to pay the $22.85 which the Boys had already spent on advertising their seances.[28]

The income from rentals vacillated drastically and each case had to be decided on its merits. Asa Hutchinson, who had rented the large hall for a concert, applied for a reduction of the price on account of the inclemency of the weather and consequent meager attendance. The Board granted a $5 reduction.[29]

The Institute had saddled itself with heavy financial responsibility, and the minutes sometimes reflect concern. The "very low condition of the Treasury would require all efforts to be made in the matter of collecting the outstanding dues." The Board frequently campaigned for new members by forgiving initiation fees to those nominated by incumbents. Nevertheless, when the house and lot adjoining the Institute building at 811 Market Street became available, the Board decided that it would be a valuable acquisition and purchased the property for rental. The twenty-six foot lot fronted Market Street and extended through to Shipley Street. The price of $5,000 was to be paid within five years.[30]

In April of 1861, the recorder made no mention of the Civil War or of the firing on Fort Sumpter, but the hostilities affected the Institute. The Board granted the large Hall to Captain Robert Lammott to drill his military company, the "Home Guard," without charge. Major R. P. Gilpin took over the south third story room to drill his company. Captain Joseph M. Barr drilled his military company in the north third story room. The Board later had to confer in regard to the $68.87 "injury sustained by the Hall, since its occupation by the troops." The tenants of the stores asked release from the payment of their first quarter's rent because of the "unsettled state of the country and the almost entire suspension of business." Delaware, a Union state, bordered Maryland, which was sympathetic to the Confederate cause, and citizens were rightly distressed. The Institute remitted the quarter's rents.[31]

The Institute resolved to "offer every facility to the Ladies' Association for the Relief of Sick & Wounded Soldiers in the prosecution of their patriotic object" during the daylight hours and at night in rare cases. Two basement rooms were rented to the quartermaster for storing military goods. The Board accepted the resignation or remitted the membership dues of members absent in the service.[32]

As the war moved to its ultimate resolution, the secretary recorded,

> The members of the Wilmington Institute assembling for their annual meeting on the day of the capture from the rebel armies of the city of Richmond and recognizing in this victory an auspicious movement towards its obtaining of an early and honourable peace, desire to make this minute of their humble thanksgiving to Almighty God for this great mercy, and of their earnest desire for a speedy and entire restoration of national unity and concord.[33]

Very shortly after this grateful communication came a sadder message. The Board of Directors of the Wilmington Institute formally expressed their sentiments in regard to the lamentable death of Abraham Lincoln, "our late beloved Chief Magistrate," and the "deplorable circumstances attending his decease."

> The death of Abraham Lincoln at any time, whether in office or out of office, would have moved the people most profoundly; but occurring as it did on the eve of a well-won and honourable peace—the glory of which belonged (under God) so largely to his genius and virtues—and at the moment of the nation's greatest confidence in his integrity and capacity, and caused, too, by the hatred of a hired and traitorous assassin, his unexpected and cruel end must produce in every loyal and humane heart feelings of the deepest awe, reverence, and affection.[34]

The Board decided that the papers relating to Lincoln and his death should be collected and donated to the Historical Society of Delaware.

The City of Wilmington grew steadily during the sixties, and the Wilmington Institute expected to keep pace and grow to one or two thousand members. Instead, the 666 membership declined somewhat. Initiation fees of $1 and annual fees of $3, and later $4 a year, may have deterred re-enrollment. Each year the committee reported the numbers and the efforts made to recruit new ones. One massive effort in the seventies took membership over 700, but any lesser effort seemed to result in steady erosion. Sometimes the numbers dipped below 500.

In 1868, the Institute claimed a membership of 560 people. The Wilmington City Directory lists the occupations of 280 of those, showing the business and mercantile connections of the members. 31 were professional men, 31 owners or officers in manufacturing firms, 41 retail merchants, 35 clerks, and 60 skilled and semi-skilled workmen. A bias in favor of business and industry shaped the membership.[35]

At the annual meeting in 1868, Col. A. H. Grimshaw took the floor and delivered some scathing criticism of the officers, resolving that decreasing membership resulted from a failure to deliver the literary lectures required by the Constitution and an insufficient number of new and popular library books. Grimshaw charged that too much was paid for salaries compared to book purchases. In the general outburst that followed, the shortage of funds caused by the repayment of the debt loomed as the important issue. J. T. Heald once again suggested a new membership drive allowing each member to propose a new member at reduced fees.[36]

The Board considered other ideas to make membership more attractive by enlarging the reading room and library, but because of financial constraints, settled on such cosmetic changes as installing matting on the floor and purchasing a large quantity of chintz to cover the Market Street wall "in pleats to within six feet of the floor," to combat the reverberation in the Hall. When all was in readiness, the Board inspected the improvements and found an improvement "both in appearance and sound."[37]

The Institute gave scholarship memberships to some young men and instituted "half tickets" allowing young people borrowing privileges, but no votes. The tickets went less well than hoped, being used only by boys whose families could and would pay anyway. Members complained of the poor apprentice boys they meant to benefit who would not "or at least do not, avail themselves of the advantages thus offered."[38]

Continued financial stress led Board members to recommend that the house adjoining the library be sold, and that a new mortgage extending the debt be negotiated so that there would be more money to purchase books. This proposal sparked a debate centered on the purpose of the library. Should its main concerns be scientific or literary? One articulate faction recommended in favor of science and against selling the house property which might well house a natural history museum and laboratory. Young people particularly were fascinated by scientific apparatus and lectures and should be taught. Besides that, several scientific organizations had deposited books and apparatus with the Institute, trusting the Board to carry out scientific designs. Such a convenient property could never be regained. The next door property was kept, and the scientific emphasis was retained. The literary lectures requested and provided for in the charter were suspended.[39]

Another basic question, faced by libraries to this day, was whether patrons should be supplied with what they wanted or what the library thought they should have. The annual report of 1868 states the purpose of the library: "to elevate the taste and to improve the intellect of the reading public." The officers felt they had "no right to lower the standard to gratify individuals," which meant buying increasing volumes of fiction.[40] Yet when this stance resulted in lack of interest, shrinking membership, and decreased income, then collections and services suffered. The members felt they must reach out to the public and sell their institution, offering popular services to keep the institution vital. This ambivalence led to constant tension between efforts to be uplifting and popular.

In the serious, uplifting mode, the officers attempted to institute more rigorous standards. After hiring a new librarian, the board members informed the current librarian, Mrs. Hennrietta W. Breese, who had served for fourteen years, that her services would no longer be required. The directors "cheerfully [bore] testimony to her fidelity as Librarian, to her punctuality and to her care of the Institute property." They declared that the change was not impelled by personal considerations, but by "the conviction that the Institute now requires the services of a Librarian upon whom shall devolve more extensive duties, which in their opinion a gentleman is most competent to perform." The growing size and value of the collection mandated someone "who makes the study of books and bibliography

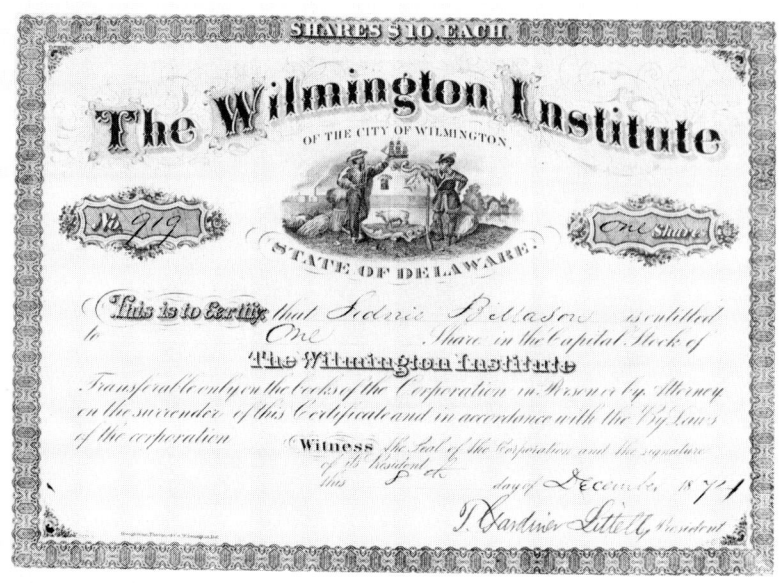

17. Stock certificate for the Wilmington Institute, 1874.

his constant employment," a person of "sound literary judgement and taste" to prepare a topical index.[41] Augustus F. Wilmans was named the new librarian.

In order to fund the purchase of sufficient new books, the Board restructured the remaining significant debt. The first mortgage of $13,000 and the eighteen $500 second mortgage bonds totaled $22,000. The First Mortgage was raised to $18,000 and $5,000 applied to the Second Mortgage, leaving $4,000 in bonds, one bond to be paid each year. This lowered the total bond repayment to $500 each year. The annual budgets of about $8,700 a year remained quite constant. A few years later the Institute sold off the property next door for $9,000 to fund building improvements.[42]

In an effort to serve the working young of the area, the Wilmington Institute offered classes for young people. Officers thought that the education of the young was central to their charter, and they had rented space to the Night School Association in 1862. In 1882, President Stansbury J. Willey proposed that the Institute contribute to the production of intelligent and skilled labor, and that classes be offered for girls as well as boys to help them support themselves. He suggested courses in mechanical drawing, architectural drawing, designing, shorthand, construction and use of tools, accounting, and simple physics and chemistry. The Board of Education offered such classes in 1885, and the prize pupils were offered free memberships in the Institute. The Institute also offered popular entertainments for "the class of young men for whom it was designed," and repaired the building to "direct and assist the rising generation to nobler aims of life."[43]

A mechanical drawing school with two classes was first opened on October 11, 1886 for fifty-seven pupils. The classes met weekly for twelve weeks in the fall. The apprentices and journeymen represented machinists, pattern-makers, car-builders, sash-makers, blacksmiths, joiners, carpenters, stone masons, draughtsmen, and other tradesmen. The students were young men from sixteen to twenty-one and on up. They were offered training, at small tuition, to supplement what was available on the job at local industries. The courses were underwritten, to some extent, by local industry, which could then hire the graduates. In 1894, 129 students attended evening sessions of the drafting school. The graduates were regarded as an "acquisition to mechanical trades of the community," and the directors began to envision a technical school.[44]

The school expanded to three classes and four, sometimes expanding in size, sometimes with disappointing response. "Few of these boys seem to desire to improve themselves," the management fretted, repeating the standard conflict. Girls were admitted to the classes in the mid 90s. The school reached a peak enrollment of about 200 with ten instructors and continued through 1902.[45]

A new Masonic Temple, the Grand Opera House, was constructed across the street in 1871 and competed for rental business. The Institute was obliged to approve the use of the Hall for dancing parties. The "private dancing sociables during the past winter have been exceedingly objectionable," the reports complained. The Hall rental receipts were down to one third of what they had been in 1871-72, and the committee was forced to rent to "minstrel troupes, panoramas, balls, etc." "We have collected as much money as we could from the property, and spent as little as we could with economy," the committee reported with weariness.[46]

THE WILMINGTON INSTITUTE.

INCORPORATED JANUARY, 1859.

Wilmington, Del April 1st 1878

Report of Rooms & Fixtures Committee.

The Committee on Rooms & Fixtures Respectfully report that they have attended to the duties of their appointment, have collected the Rents as promptly as possible, Spent as little for Repairs as or as consistent with true Economy, and submit their results as follows

Collected Rents of Stores & Rooms	$3 035.25	2833.10	
" " Hall	1527.53	1576.03	
Total	$4 562.78	4409.13	
Yet due & uncollected	$ 530.25	683.9	

Respectfully submitted

Mahlon M Childs
Saml D Smith
Geo. A. Elliott

Committee.

18. Report of the Rooms and Fixtures Committee from the Minutes of the Executive Committee of the Wilmington Institute at its regular meeting, April 1, 1878.

Another gloomy financial aspect was the fact that the library was required to pay taxes which often amounted to an eighth of its annual income, twice what could be afforded to spend on books. Public libraries were not required to pay taxes, but the Wilmington Institute could not afford to go public. Caught in this difficult financial dilemma, the officers expressed frustration. W. S. Auchincloss, President of the Board of Directors, stated the case in 1877.

Many states in our Union take the greatest delight in establishing free public libraries, in their principal cities, and support them with unstinted measure. Such a course exerts the most powerful influence toward the repression of crime, and teaches the juvenile portion of the community habits of order, politeness, and industry, in addition to the good they derive from a well-stocked library. A ten-fold result is eventually felt from such influences, and the demand for large police forces, reformatory schools, and prisons, is diminished. Not so in Delaware, one of the original thirteen States![47]

As no help was forthcoming elsewhere, the Institute decided to commemorate its centennial year in 1888 by raising money to pay off the $21,000 encumbrance on the building, and relieved of that burden, become a free library. The committee meeting under the direction of Job H. Jackson set a goal of $25,000 and set to work. The campaign failed. The next year Jackson came back with pledges of $8,835 and the suggestion that a new committee be named.[48]

In the thirty-one years since the Institute had been established, the membership of the society had remained the same. The population and wealth of the city had tripled; the number of volumes had tripled; the circulation of the Institute had doubled. But the membership was only 663.[49] Wilmington remained a city without a college, with crowded public schools, with few educational opportunities, and no free public library.

The library was slowly paying off debts, looking in vain for some of the considerable gifts of books or money which had been bestowed upon other libraries. The Board considered selling the building, clearing the debt, and building anew. The library had grown, incorporating other organizations, acquiring books, moving into larger quarters. But it remained a very small operation, available to less than

RULES AND REGULATIONS

FOR THE USE OF THE

Library and Reading Room,

OF THE WILMINGTON INSTITUTE.

ART. I.—Library Room when open and closed.

The Library room to be open daily from 8 A. M. to 10 P. M. Sundays, the Fourth of July, Thanksgiving Day and Christmas, excepted.

ART. II.—Who shall use the Library.

The use of the Library Room is restricted to members.

Any member possessing a ticket, shall have the privilege of introducing a non-resident or a lady.

The Librarian may require the ticket of membership to be shown, and every person upon whom the requisition is made, shall comply or leave the room.

Privilege of Strangers.

Strangers and non-residents shall have the privilege of the room for a period of thirty days, but shall not be entitled to take any books from the Library Room.

ART. III.—How non-members may obtain Books.

Persons not members may obtain Books on the account of members upon the presentation of a written order, or of said Member's Ticket. Non-compliance with this rule shall justify the withholding of Books by the Librarian.

ART. IV.—Number of Books Loaned, and Rules respecting it.

Each member is entitled to take from the Library one Folio or Quarto, or Two Octavo or Duodecimo volumes at the same time; provided, that the two volumes shall not form parts of different sets of books. When two volumes of the same set have been loaned both must be returned before another can be taken out.

ART. V.—Time for which Books are Loaned.

Folios and Quartos may be retained for a period of six weeks. Octavos may be retained for four weeks, and Duodecimo for three weeks.

ART. VI.—Rules Respecting New Books.

New books or books which have been in the Library for less time than three months, shall be labelled *New Books*, and can be loaned for but one-half the periods designated in Article V, and but one such volume shall be issued to a member at one time.

[The Library Regulations have failed to designate the *New Books*, and misunderstanding and ill-feeling have sometime arisen upon the reclamation of fines, when books have been kept out over time, from want of knowing that they were of the class of " New Books." The designation by a special label, upon the expiration of the three months, is the plan adopted in some Libraries and seems to be the most feasible in the present instance.]

ART. VII.—How extra Volumes may be Loaned.

Extra volumes may be taken out and retained for four weeks, on payment in advance of ten cents per week for each volume; provided, always, that this privilege shall not extend to "New Books," or to works which are in considerable demand.

ART. VIII.—Times for detention of Books.

Books retained longer than the periods specified, without renewal, are subject to a fine of 5 cents per week and fraction of a week, per volume.

ART. IX.—Rule respecting renewal of Books.

New Books, are not in any case subject to renewal. Other Books may be renewed once only; provided, they have not been kept out longer than the time permitted by the regulations.

ART. X.—Books to be returned to the Librarian.

The Librarian may require a Book to be produced previous to renewing it; and all Books when returned, are to be handed to the Librarian for examination.

ART. XI.—Penalty for Detention of Books.

Upon the expiration of the time limited by the regulations for the return of Books, they shall be reclaimed by notice from the Librarian, and if not returned within ten days after such notice, they shall be replaced at the expense of the borrower.

ART. XII.—Penalty for Loss or Damage of Books.

Books lost or injured shall be replaced at the borrower's expense, and if the book or books form part of a set, the whole set shall be paid for or replaced by the borrower, who shall then be entitled to the remaining volumes as his property.

ART. XIII.—Penalty for taking Books from Library without Registry.

Any member who shall take a Book from the Library without having it charged in the Register, shall forfeit his right to the use of the Library.

ART XIV.—Librarian not to pre-engage Books.

The Librarian is not, under any circumstances at liberty to reserve books for members, or in any way to use partiality in loaning them.

ART XV.—Rule respecting admission of Minors to Library Room.

Minors under fifteen years of age, shall not be considered as entitled to visit the Library unless accompanied by older members, or to obtain or return a book for a member, and when there, shall not be allowed to handle the books, papers or periodicals, unless by consent obtained from the Librarian. Upon any abuse of privilege accorded, they shall be *expelled* from the room.

ART. XVI.—Rule respecting unbound Volumes and Periodicals, &c.

Unbound Periodicals and Pamphlets shall not, in any case, be taken from the Library, nor shall the papers be removed from the files.

How Books of Reference may be Loaned.

Books designated by the Board of Directors as works of reference, shall not be taken from the Library without special permission of the Library Committee, and on leaving with the Librarian a deposit in money, the amount, and the time for which the loan shall be made, to be determined by the said Committee.

ART. XVII.—Loud talking Prohibited.

Conversation must be conducted in a low whisper.

ART. XVIII—Other Acts Prohibited.

The following acts are positively prohibited :—

Smoking ; unnecessary noise ; defacing fixtures or furniture; sitting or lying on the tables or window seats; spitting elsewhere than in the spittoons ; throwing nut-shells or other refuse on the floor ; bringing dogs into the room.

Rules to be Enforced.

Any improper conduct in the room or violation of the rules, is to be reported immediately to some officer of the Institute-with the name of the offender.

N. B.—Members are respectfully requested to exercise a proper discretion in the use of the late papers, so that all who desire it may have the privilege of reading the news.

19. Rules and regulations for the use of the library and reading room of the Wilmington Institute Free Library, about 1880.

1,000 citizens, those who desired to use its books and could afford its dues. Still the library survived when other groups went under. Frequently financially strapped because of taxes, debts, and delinquent dues, needing to replace worn books and buy new ones, the library struggled on.

FOUR

The Wilmington Institute Free Library, 1894 to 1915

T HE MODERN LIBRARY MOVEMENT BEGAN WITH THE PASSAGE OF LAWS ENABLING LOCAL GOVERNMENTAL UNITS TO LEVY TAXES FOR THE SUPPORT OF PUBLIC LIBRARIES. IN 1849, NEW HAMPSHIRE WAS THE FIRST STATE TO AUTHORIZE TOWNS TO APPROPRIATE MONEY FOR THE ESTABLISHMENT AND MAINTENANCE OF PUBLIC LIBRARIES. MASSACHUSETTS FOLlowed in 1851, and Maine in 1854.

The industrial revolution had produced large cities with populations of uneducated immigrants, and education seemed the best way to secure the country against destructive change. The native-born Americans recognized that publicly supported education would socialize new citizens in the ways of democracy, and immigrants looked to education to get ahead politically and economically. The relation between knowledge and virtue was drawn; universal free public education would solve problems.

The American free public library developed in response to these changing times. The public recognized the limits of voluntarism. In the late Jacksonian period people realized that society needed governmental intervention to promote general welfare.

Another significant development was the founding of the American Library Association in 1876 which began to codify standards and circulate library literature, benefitting libraries nationally. The wide experience of others helped each local library adopt positive methods. The officers of the Wilmington Institute supported the ALA and welcomed the chance to become acquainted with other libraries.[1]

Andrew Carnegie's beneficence cannot be overrated. Carnegie gave lavishly in many directions, but his gift of library buildings to communities has probably had the greatest impact on the most people. He began funding libraries in 1881, and, by 1920, he had spent $50,000,000 on 2,500 buildings. Carnegie justified this largesse in a statement which epitomizes the reverent, saving power attributed to libraries in the late nineteenth century.

I choose free libraries as the best agencies for improving the masses of the people, because they give nothing for nothing. They only help those who help themselves. They never pauperize. They reach the aspiring, and open to these the chief treasures of the world—those stored up in books. A taste for reading drives out lower tastes. [2]

Some cities did not want his money, tainted by the hard conditions of the steel mills. Others were grateful for the marble temples which provided opportunities for their young.

Apparently the first free library in the United States was in Peterborough, N. H. Other collections and institutions had many of

20. The Wilmington Institute Building at the corner of 8th and Market Streets, 1905.

46

the trappings of such an institution, but it was at Peterborough in 1833 that all the elements came together for the first time. An institution was founded by a town with the deliberate purpose of creating a free library, open without restriction to the whole community, supported by public funds. This pattern, once created, has not changed markedly in the 150 years since.

New Hampshire's state law for public libraries in July 1849 empowered any town to "raise and appropriate money to procure books, maps, charts, periodicals, and other publications, for the establishment and perpetual maintenance" of a public library, to buy land and erect buildings, and to pay workers. These libraries should be free to every inhabitant for the "general diffusion of intelligence." Massachusetts' law was enacted in 1851, and by 1854 the state had ten free public libraries.[3]

The Boston Public Library began modestly in 1854. By then New York City had opened its library, the benefaction of the Astor fortune. Boston, stung by the fear that it might fall behind in literary matters as well as commerce, was moved to act quickly.[4]

Wilmington was far from the library forefront by then. When the Boston and New York free libraries sprang into being, the Wilmington Library Company had not yet merged with the Young Men's Association, become the Wilmington Institute, nor erected the building at Eighth and Market Streets.

The officers of the Wilmington Institute discussed opening their doors as a free library. They wanted the library made available to anyone who would use it, and they believed that lowering or eliminating the membership dues, in that day of free libraries, was the way to proceed. The Board members considered the matter repeatedly over the years, but they needed dues and fees to keep the library going. The Board regularly discussed restructuring the debt or selling the building so as to be able to lend books free.[5] The annual reports wistfully hoped that a major benefactor would come on the scene, and in 1892 the longed for angel came forth.

William P. Bancroft, a successful Quaker industrialist, had frequented the library in his youth. He remembered reading as a boy in the old Town Hall and in the second story of the market house at Fourth and Market Streets. He was a cardholder at Eighth and Market Streets.[6]

21. **William Poole Bancroft, 1835-1928, the benefactor who made the Wilmington Institute Free Library possible. Courtesy, Historical Society of Delaware.**

On a western journey, Bancroft had been impressed with the beautiful free public libraries which the gifts of Andrew Carnegie had caused to rise. Bancroft enlisted a colleague to collect statistical information about the libraries and presented the information to the Wilmington Institute, suggesting plans of public support to substitute for annual dues and Hall rental. Bancroft proposed to make the library and reading room free, in exchange for which he would make himself responsible for the cancellation of the debt of about $20,000. His significant letter, which was read to the Board on June 12, 1893, some four months after it was written, follows.

2nd mo., 23, 1893

Vincent G. Hazard, President
The Wilmington Institute

I feel much interested in the endeavor to secure through The Wilmington Institute a large free library, the means of the Institute to be supplemented by annual contribution from the city. I should like to see the library and reading rooms free to all; and still not less, *but more* useful to those who are now Institute stockholders than at present.

I believe it will promote the object for you to be able to say that the old debt of the Institute will be met by contributions; and while there are many who will be willing to help, the *assurance should be given without delay*. I, therefore, hereby guarantee that from the time the library and reading rooms shall be made free to all citizens of Wilmington who will observe such regulations as the managers may make, with satisfactory assurance that they will be maintained free, the interest on the present debt will be discharged. I believe the net amount of the debt is about $20,000.

Respectfully thy friend,
William P. Bancroft.

Wilmington Institute,

N. W. Cor. Eighth and Market Streets.

— • ◄ • • • —

A SHARE OF STOCK,

Entitling the Holder to use of Library, Reading Room, and
Literary and Scientific Lectures, is subject to a

Semi-Annual payment of Two Dollars.
The Nominal cost of Shares is Ten Dollars.

THE LIBRARY

Contains over Twelve Thousand Volumes, to which additions
are made as rapidly as the funds of the Institute will allow.

Open Every Day from 8 A. M. to 10 P. M. (except
June, July, and August, 9 P. M.)

THE READING ROOM

Is now supplied with about fifty newspapers and periodicals, the
number being increased as rapidly as possible.

22. Page taken from the 21st Annual Report, Wilmington Institute,
April, 1878.

49

This gift renewed library purpose and service, and Bancroft's "liberality and amiable pertinacity in the work"[7] insured a future for a once again ailing institution. The officers were particularly appreciative as Bancroft, who lived out by his mills in Rockford, was not even a citizen of the City of Wilmington.

The change to a free library was brought about by two acts of the State Legislature, on April 24 and April 25, 1893.[8] Bancroft negotiated the six City ordinances necessary to provide for a per capita tax and the payment to the library. The Mayor and City Council authorized the payment of one and a half cents for each inhabitant to the Wilmington Institute, providing for a popular, civic financial base. As Bancroft retired the library debt, the owners of 369 shares of common stock and fourteen life shares voluntarily assigned their shares to Security Trust and Safe Deposit Company in trust for the benefit of the free library and free reading rooms.[9]

The last meeting of the Wilmington Institute Executive Committee took place on June 24, 1893. The Board of Managers came into being that evening, and the library charter was amended in October of that year to give power to the group of sixteen managers: the Mayor, the President of City Council, the Chairman of the finance committee of City Council, the President of the Board of Education, and the Superintendent of Public Schools, all of the City of Wilmington, and ten other persons to be elected by the stockholders of the Wilmington Institute. This largely self-perpetuating group has managed the library since that day.

The Wilmington Institute Free Library, virtually debt-free, with a promising future financial base, renovated the building and opened its doors to the public on February 12, 1894. The Board of Managers still rented out stores and rooms which provided operating income in addition to the financial support from the City. In preparation for greater activity, the books were moved into the Hall which became the new Reading Room. The former reading room was immediately filled with students from No. 9 School who met there until their own building was ready. Within two or three months the cardholders increased from 700 to 7000.

For the next twenty years Bancroft sustained the library by further contributions. The city appropriation paid the cost for local residents, but Bancroft bore the cost of facilities used by people outside of

23. Rockford Branch, opened in 1896.

Wilmington. After paying a lump sum each year for these library patrons, he donated stock worth $20,000 for an endowment for library expenses for those from out of the city.[10] In 1896, he opened a Rockford Branch of the Wilmington Free Institute to which the firm of Jos. Bancroft and Sons Co. regularly contributed.

After the library became free, a subtle change in library management is evident in the reports. The long, anguished accounts of the presidents, wrestling with the finances and purposes of the institution, give way to brisk reports by the librarians concentrating on services, circulation, and outreach. The advent of the free library coincides with the change from a voluntary to a professional institution. The librarians began to serve for longer periods.

In 1895, the librarian could report that $3,000 had been spent for books, far in excess of the amounts spent in previous years. Cardholders totaled 9,127, fifteen times the number in former days. The library held subscriptions for 155 periodicals, including twenty-two daily papers.[11]

By 1899, after five years as a Free Library, the officers could report "such a growth and such an evident appreciation on the part of the public as to warrant expression of great gratification." The operating budget had virtually doubled from the days before the library was free, from about $8,000 to about $15,000.[12]

The largest growth was among young patrons. In the past, people who thought twice about paying membership fees themselves, thought three times about paying such funds for their children. Now every family member took a card. The children's corner in the library was beautified with pictures and object lessons.[13] Library policy was to have multiples of popular books rather than copies of every book available, with emphasis on good literature. The children's favorite books in 1902 were collections of Longfellow's poems; and the library possessed, in various juvenile editions, 105 copies of his work. The children's room was soon too busy for story hours and too small for enough books.[14]

In a constant outreach effort, the librarian began sending enriching materials directly to the schools. The library deposited over a thousand volumes at twenty-eight schools in 1901. These books were intended for home circulation, and the reports note with satisfaction that students were reading these books to their parents and siblings.

24. The Children's Room, at the building at 8th and Market Streets, 1910. At right is Mary Maull, children's librarian.

Each spring the staff gathered up the collections, repaired and replaced worn books, and returned them in the fall. In 1905, the librarians began regular visits to the schools to introduce young patrons to library services.[15]

Collections were issued to nine playground sites for story hours and home use. The librarians tried all avenues to interest young people in reading, though they found somewhat perplexing the girls who wanted only love stories and the boys who would only read detective fiction.[16]

25. Arthur L. Bailey, 1867-1940, the guiding spirit of the Wilmington Library who served as librarian from 1904 to 1940.

Men were encouraged to use the library too. Soon after Arthur Low Bailey became librarian in 1904, he began a special interest department, appealing to working men to use the library for their work in the "useful arts" or "applied science." Bailey placed pieces in the newspapers noting the library's excellent collections on engineering, railroading, electricity, and agriculture. Usage increased, and in a few years Bailey could rightly claim that workers had used the collections to pass civil service exams, thereby increasing their pay and garnering promotions.[17]

Bailey, who had been born in Methuen, Massachusetts in 1867, and who spent thirty-seven years as the guiding spirit of the Wilmington Free Institute Library, probably exercised the most powerful influence over the institution. Known as "Books" Bailey, he served on the board of the American Library Association and authored a book on library management. His imaginative energies left an enduring legacy. He organized the traveling library for rural New Castle County and opened branch libraries. In an effort to document the

26. The loan desk, about 1900, with, left to right, Emma Eckman, Florence Shepherd, and Jean Ogle.

state's heritage, Bailey began to collect Delaware materials, including ephemeral reports, catalogues, and annuals of businesses, churches, and civic associations. He sent out letters to organizations requesting that publications be deposited in the library.[18]

Bailey began the library's collection of Delawareana which has been its great pride and burden for many years. He aimed to gather important Delaware imprints and historical works and purchased valuable 18th and 19th century volumes during his tenure. New Delaware books and authors were added to the collection as published.

He also collected information. Bailey began an index file of typed cards on Delaware subjects. He had librarians clip newspapers for Delaware stories and had them mount thousands of clippings in scrapbooks. He also had them index the state's major reference books and periodicals of local interest for a massive Delaware master index. All of this material proved invaluable in answering the many questions relating the state that were asked each week.[19] His early index is still valuable many years later.

Another of his schemes was to collect pictures, mount them and circulate them to schools. Teachers borrowed from the 7,000 pictures

54

available. Additional pictures were mounted steadily.[20]

To satisfy the demand for popular, new books, the library instituted a Duplicate Pay Collection. Clients paid five cents each to borrow these multiple copies of popular books which became free as soon as the accumulated nickels added up to the selling price. In one year the library added 345 books to the best selling collection in this way.[21]

Individual home book delivery was offered via messenger for five cents per book. Western Union provided the service by contract to the library. Though popular on rainy days, this convenient service was discontinued for lack of use.[22]

27. The Wilmington Institute Building, about 1923.

The library began service to the blind, supplying books in the Moon and Braille systems. Librarians worked with a blind teacher who visited shut-ins and taught them to read and to do manual tasks. A room in the library was set aside for services to the blind, before an agency to provide services to the blind was set up on Delaware Avenue.[23]

The library extended hours by opening to the public on Sunday afternoons. Despite lukewarm response, the Board continued Sunday hours. The staff prepared recommended lists of books by subject; they sent out letters and gave talks to interested groups; they sent lists of new books to the newspapers to be published; they prepared ads to be flashed onto movie screens. Anything they could think of to generate public awareness, they did.[24]

Public demand led to the purchase of 100 volumes in Polish. The library soon bought an additional 100. A Polish language station, or small branch, was set up at Chestnut and Adams Streets.[25]

All this activity strained the capacity of the building. In 1908, $5,300 was spent for books which required new shelving. Carpenters added a balcony inside the reading room, later a gallery, and finally cut a hole through the floor and put up shelves in the room below.[26] The library branched out.

Besides the collections lodged with the various schools, the librarians began to put books at other locations around the City to encourage convenient usage by more citizens. Books were placed at a community center called the People's Settlement. The first Brandywine branch, an experimental station with 200 books, was set up in a grocery store at 1908 Market Street. Deposit stations at the Woodlawn Club and the West End Reading Room opened next, followed by the installation of books at the YMCA and Planet Mills Manufacturing.[27]

Some experiments were not successful. The People's Settlement station was closed, as was the Brandywine station and a "Colored Settlement" station which operated briefly. But progress came from other directions. The stone Brandywine Academy building, owned by the City, and dating from 1798, was given to the library for a new Brandywine Branch. The city renovated the outdated structure, and the branch there opened October 14, 1915. The library opened stations at Hagley Community House and Olivet Presbyterian Church.

To increase usage of the Rockford Branch, library assistants made home calls on potential patrons.[28]

All of these programs were part of the militant effort to increase awareness of the library's holdings and thereby the use of the books. The staff aimed to meet the needs of all citizens in the city. But once again this was to be accomplished by raising, rather than by lowering, standards. Librarian Bailey began a program allowing clients to take out two books at a time, as long as one was non-fiction. He counted this program a great success, as "a very perceptible improvement in the character of the circulation at once became apparent." But for Bailey, circulation was not the major end. He noted that he could increase circulation vastly by "a lowering of the standard upon which books are admitted to the shelves, a direct catering to the demands of the moment," and other compromises with quality. The Wilmington Institute took seriously its mission to improve the masses.[29]

Such a progressive library required a more spacious and aesthetically pleasing building. Bailey complained of "an unattractive building and cheap furnishings" which reflected poorly on the very good work done there. President Vincent G. Hazard wanted a new building "attractive in outward appearance and commensurate with the fitness of things." Small fires in 1913 and 1914 reminded everyone that the building was dangerously flammable.[30]

The Wilmington Institute, though shabby and outdated, still rented out enough space to earn seven or eight thousand dollars a year. The Board members noted that they would be very happy to leave the old building and to escape all the real estate management necessary to rent the space, but they saw no way the library could manage without the funds of the tenants. They sought increased City support.

An act passed by the Wilmington Council back on March 26, 1903 had said that the Mayor and Council of Wilmington must pay to the Institute "$50 per year for every $1,000 bequeathed or donated" for the support of free libraries and reading rooms, not to exceed $5,000 yearly. The City of Wilmington was then paying $5,000 in support each year.

The Board of Managers proposed an additional agreement for the City to pay fifty dollars per year in matching funds per thousand dollars raised, up to two hundred thousand dollars, which the library would then raise to erect a new building. This $10,000 would be in addition to the $5,000 already being received. The new $10,000 in income would take the place of the rental income.[31] On November 19, 1913, the City Council passed a measure to pay up to $10,000 additional income.

With $15,000 of City support guaranteed, the library managers felt that they could afford to give up the building rentals. The Board began to plan a new building, raise money, consider sites, and think about moving up Market Street once again.

FIVE

The New Building, 1915 to 1924

N O DELAWARE LIBRARIES BENEFITTED FROM THE PROGRAMS OF ANDREW CARNEGIE. CITY GOVERNMENTS THAT ENJOYED THE GIFT OF BUILDINGS DONATED BY ANDREW CARNEGIE WERE EXPECTED TO PAY YEARLY MAINTENANCE SUMS EQUAL TO TEN PER CENT OF THE VALUE OF THE BUILDINGS. THE WILMINGTON INSTITUTE COULD PERSUADE THE CITY GOV- ernment to pay the library only five percent of the cost of the library, and only up to library donations of $300,000, for an annual subsidy of $15,000. Wilmington did not qualify for the gift of a Carnegie library building because the City support was too low.[1]

The Board realized that no building money would be forthcoming from the State or from the City government; the members would have to raise funds locally from public spirited citizens. Yet they needed a larger and more commodious building to house "our really good and efficient collection of books, etc., a building that will be attractive in outward appearance and commensurate with the fitness of things, and more nearly on a par with the strides and advancement of the city in other directions."[2]

The old building at Eighth and Market Streets had served the community well, but it was "combustible" and no longer suitable. A city like Wilmington needed a dignified, artistic, and fire-proof building. Librarian Arthur L. Bailey reported to the Board that the present library held 77,000 volumes with room for fifty-six adults and thirty-six children to sit down, and with no room for expansion. Bailey estimated that the library needed shelf-space for 150,000 volumes and sitting room for 300 people. His extremely conservative estimate for such a building was $30,000. The Board had much more ambitious plans in mind, a landmark building on what was to become Rodney Square.[3]

Wilmington's center was moving steadily up the hill on Market Street. By 1900, activity had reached 10th and Market Streets, where the Court House Square would become Rodney Square, a suitable city center. The three du Pont cousins built headquarters for the DuPont Company on Market between Tenth and Eleventh Streets. The DuPont Building rose in six sections, completed between 1907 and 1931. The new Public Building for city and county governments along the King Street side was completed in 1917. By the spring of 1915, the square had been designated as a memorial to Caesar

28. Tenth and Market Streets in 1922, the site of the First Presbyterian Church with adjoining cemetery prior to the construction of the Wilmington Library.

Rodney, and the equestrian statue by James Kelley was unveiled in 1923. A handsome Federal Building, replacing the McComb-Winchester mansion, was dedicated in 1937. Early on, the Board of Managers had spotted the fourth side of this square as a suitable place for the new library.[4]

The site, Tenth Street between Market and King Streets, contained early and later buildings owned by the First Presbyterian Church as well as a cemetery. The first small building, built in 1740, had been leased to the Historical Society of Delaware.[5] The Library Board entered into negotiations with the church as early as 1913, fearing that the development of the square would raise prices exorbitantly.[6]

62

The leadership of the church was willing to listen. The church suffered from financial problems, and the trustees had considered leasing the church property. But there was opposition to the idea of dealing with a business which would seem crass. Serious opposition would arise before a commercial office building supplanted a cemetery. The idea of a beautiful new library, however, would encourage public pride. The Library hoped to manage a lease at an annual $9-10,000, figuring the value of the land at about $250,000 with about 3.5% paid annually for ground rent.[7]

The managers thought they could sell the Eighth and Market Street property for between $180,000 and $200,000. Then, if they could raise $300,000 from a public subscription for the building, they would have enough for an ambitious library. The City of Wilmington's annual donation of $15,000 could be used for the building.[8]

As it later worked out, the old library building was eventually sold to John Govatos for $325,000, a great deal more than had originally been anticipated, on May 31, 1919. Govatos, the purchaser, agreed to pay $50,000 to seal the agreement and $50,000 on the receipt of the deed which was to be within seven years from the date of the agreement, when the

29. Pierre S. duPont, 1870-1954. He bought the land for the present building in 1915 for $225,000. Photo by Brooks Studio, Wilmington, Delaware.

library vacated the premises.[9] The old building was eventually torn down and replaced by a yellow brick Kresge dime store with the company name marked out on the back and front facades. A Rite Aid Discount Pharmacy currently occupies the building.

The library's second major benefactor, Pierre S. du Pont, was brought into the library scheme in 1914. "I am greatly interested," du Pont told John P. Nields, a member of the Board of Managers of the library for almost forty years, and also a lawyer and later a judge, "and propose to take some definite action as soon as I am able to give time to it." When du Pont had some time, he agreed to pay the cost of the first ten years of lease to the Presbyterian Church.[10]

As negotiations moved along, Pierre S. du Pont raised his original offer and agreed to contribute $200,000 toward the $245,000 needed to buy, rather than lease, the property. He also agreed to contribute an additional $45,000 to the public fund to buy land and erect the building. DuPont was willing to acknowledge the $45,000 donation, but wanted the $200,000 kept quiet.[11]

He authorized the publication by the Board of Managers of a statement in the public press as follows:

> The donor (of the site) has asked us to proceed at once with the campaign for the building and has stated that in making the gift (of the site) he expects the campaign to begin at once."[12]

The campaigners set their sights at $325,000, and under the direction of Edgar T. Honey and with L. Scott Townsend as treasurer, raised the money by popular subscription. They concentrated their efforts in seven days, April 12-20, 1916.[13] A leaflet addressed "To Every Citizen of Wilmington," noted that the city had never had an adequate building and that the public library was fundamentally democratic and universal, providing for all classes, ages, and conditions. The leaflet noted that a magnificent site had been donated by a public spirited citizen and that city revenues would provide $15,000 a year if the campaign reached its goal.

The old library, the leaflet went on to note, is "unattractive in appearance, inadequate in its facilities, and is not fire-proof." Many valuable books were irreplaceable. The working rooms were small and inadequate as well as unattractive.[14] Goldey's Commercial College,

A New Library Building

$325,000

IN SEVEN DAYS
A P R I L 1 2 - 2 0

WILMINGTON INSTITUTE
FREE LIBRARY

HEADQUARTERS
HOTEL DU PONT
TELEPHONE No. 325,000

30. Front page of four page appeal, April 1916. Wilmington Institute papers. Courtesy, Historical Society of Delaware.

the main tenant, was moving out. The swift campaign raised more than the required $325,000, in just five days.

If only the building could have begun then. But the beginning of construction was postponed. The actual funds had to be gathered in, and the graves needed to be relocated in various other cemeteries, at a cost of about $40,000.[15]

During 1917 and 1918 the Board collected building pledges and invested the sums. It was 1919 before $299,000 in securities was in hand. The Board of Managers saw to clearing the site. In June of 1918, they decided to proceed with final architectural drawings.[16]

Meanwhile, librarian Arthur L. Bailey had been working on a design in conference with Alfred M. Githens and Edward L. Tilton, the New York architects who had been chosen to design the building.[17] The architects were asked to develop three separate sets of plans from which to choose. Their favorite design was also the unanimous choice of the committee. The shape of the lot, 200 feet long and 90 feet deep, with good light on three sides and fairly good light at the rear, called for an unusual building. The architects proposed to put the books downstairs, to take advantage of the natural light.

The outbreak of World War I seriously delayed library construction, but influenced library activities in many other ways. The staff cooperated with all war organizations and helped in the food campaign by supplying books on gardening and canning. The librarians added selected military and naval works, and also some books on preparing for emergencies. In 1918, the Board of Health closed the building for the month of October because of the influenza epidemic.

In addition, the library collected 5,000 volumes and $13,000 for books for servicemen. John P. Nields issued a flyer requesting that used volumes be donated. He indicated another concern as well.

Your books… may be the means of converting Bolshevists into good Americans, and combatting the radical element in our midst by giving them welcome truths to think about. *Every good book on America is a bulwark for the business interests of our city.* [18]

The librarians began "work with foreigners," hoping to "help mould" immigrants into good citizens. Many of these speakers of foreign languages were too old for school, and as no night school was available, the library could provide help needed. The librarian proposed collections in Russian, Hebrew, and Yiddish.[19]

Arthur Bailey took many of the donated books to Camp Meade where he spent three months setting up a servicemen's library.[20] After the armistice, circulation rose 25%, and the library supplied information on job hunting to demobilized veterans.

When the war was over, the Board of Managers was eager to begin the new building, but inflated construction prices caused concern. The Board reported that "The New Building project is a victim of the

PROPOSED DESIGN OF A NEW PUBLIC LIBRARY BUILDING FOR WILMINGTON
TO BE ERECTED ON TENTH STREET BETWEEN MARKET AND KING STREETS

COMPLIMENTS OF
THE BOARD OF MANAGERS OF THE PUBLIC LIBRARY

31. Proposed design for a new public building for Wilmington to be erected on Tenth street between Market and King Streets.

changed conditions prevailing" and the "consequent altered standards of value." Should building begin at once, at high prices while stocks were devalued, or should the Board wait for ten years or so for normality to return?

The building itself would probably cost $500,000 if construction proceeded at once, and the Board had only $300,000 in hand. Nields appealed once again to du Pont, asking him for additional funds and to take over the library securities at their face value.[21] This time duPont refused. He favored City support, allowing that he might be willing to do more after the City had done its share.

Nields went to the City and requested a bond issue for the required $200,000. He began a major campaign for City support, producing a survey comparing Wilmington's library to those of thirty-

32. John P. Nields, who served on the Board of Managers for forty years beginning in 1894 and was the president from 1921 to 1943.

three other comparable cities. Of the group, twenty-nine had greater per capita city appropriations. Fifteen had larger per capita circulation, but all of those had larger per capita city appropriations.[22]

Nields was gratified when the City of Wilmington agreed to appropriate funds to help with library construction. The City purchased the lot donated by du Pont from the library for the $200,000 and authorized a bond issue for that amount. The $200,000 would go toward the cost of the building, and all other Institute income would go toward maintainance. The City would lease the land to the Institute as long as a library was in operation there.[23] When Nields was able to inform du Pont that the city had agreed to issue the $200,000 worth of bonds at 5% and make up any deficiency on discounted bonds, du Pont congratulated him on a job well done.[24]

Finally, it was time to go ahead with the building. "We certainly want it, the public asks for it, and labor needs an opportunity to go to work again," the report noted. Prices were falling, and the Board was willing to modify cherished designs to get on with the project. The architects, Tilton and Githens, revised the drawings and specifications made some five years previously to bring the cost of the building down to the $500,000 available. The funding settled, the library advertised for bids and accepted that of the DuPont Engineering Company, which proposed to do the job for $386,666, a low enough bid that most of the original plans could be followed. The total contract price was $424,001.[25]

When the cornerstone was laid on March 4, 1922, Mayor LeRoy Harvey remarked that the day began "a new era in the life of an institution which has been ministering to the intellectual and moral needs of the people of our city since 1788." He concluded with the motto of the library.

"Per manus lampas tradatur." We have received the lamp from those who have gone before. Who can measure the influence shed by its rays for 134 years on our citizens? Let it be borne aloft by us as we pass, and let it be handed on, trimmed and brightly burning, to those who come after us, eager to assume our duties and traditions as Wilmingtonians.[26]

The work of the architects proceeded with great care. When some of the managers complained of the long construction period, Tilton and Githens responded that the carving of the limestone was moving ahead in New York in a cautious manner. "We would never cease to regret if any inferiority were obtained from endeavoring simply to complete the building a few weeks sooner."[27]

The Wilmington Institute Free Library was closed for three weeks, and the old building was vacated in haste by April 25. On May 5, 1923, the new building was dedicated. "Spaciousness, light, beauty and convenience," met the proud and wondering public. A lovely little statue of Hebe serenely regarded the visitors.[28]

The building represented the latest thinking in library construction. The children's library on King Street had chairs for 100 and shelves for 15,000 books. The two tiers of steel stacks under the first floor had a capacity for 350,000 books and the main floor reference and reading-room held an additional 50,000 volumes.

At the ceremonies, Pierre S. du Pont stressed that the new building was merely a shell and that the real library was housed within it. He modestly gave the true credit for the library to William P. Bancroft and said that libraries were beautiful monuments to

33. The cornerstone laying of the new library building, March 4, 1922.

immortal remains as cemeteries were monuments to mortal remains. Nields described the library in modern terms.

This library is a distributing plant located at the center of traffic. By distributing scientific and practical information it should increase the efficiency of business men and of industrial workers. In other words, it should yield a cash dividend to the people for providing its maintenance.[29]

The architect Alfred M. Githens noted at the ceremony that the arrangement differed from other libraries in being an open interior with few partitions and one large room opening into another, a very modern floor plan. The general impression, according to the architects, is "of openness and of light, strong, flooding, brilliant light."[30]

The colors are strong, but not shocking. The color is reminiscent of the bright colors originally common in classical buildings, and used, as indicated by the architect, according to the surest precedent.

Eclectic in a series of classical styles, using the harmonious vocabulary of many structures, the building featured Roman Ionic columns on the exterior, black Greek Doric columns with red and

34. The North Front of the Wilmington Public Library, Wilmington, Delaware, before the shrubbery against the base was in place. Edward L. Tilton and Alfred Morton Githens, Associated Architects.

35. The north front of the Wilmington Library, from *Architecture, the Professional Architectural Monthly,* July, 1923.

cream colored Pompeiian capitals on the first floor, and yellow Roman Ionic columns on the second floor.

The architecture was styled *Roman Imperial.* Githens noted that much of the Roman work was done by Greek artisans who brought their skills to Roman architecture. As architectural styles flowed from each other, artisans would use aspects from all that they knew.

The interior sculptured frieze, representing a procession of Athenians travelling on foot and horse to the Parthenon to celebrate a festival held every four years to honor Athena, was cast from the Elgin Marbles taken from the Athenian Parthenon.

For the facade, the architects had "seized on the possibility of a great wall surface with a gorgeous doorway in the midst, high as the ceiling would permit." They designed the sliding doors to be nineteen feet high. This classic construction, solid in the center and open at the ends, was without precedent. The facade of the building, rich in symbolic detail, was described by Alfred M. Githens in a letter to Edgar M. Hoopes, Jr., chairman of the Building Committee.[32]

Designs are carved to represent the official corporate seal of the Library and its Latin motto: *Per manus Lampas Tradatur,* which translates to mean "From hand to hand is passed the Torch of Learning." The seal is flanked by books festooned with Delaware's own peach-branches. Grapevines, representing the fruition of learn-

71

36. The circulation department as seen from the mezzanine in 1923, with Abby Mack at the front desk and Caroline Philips at the charging desk. Photo by John Wallace Gilies, New York.

ing, surround the doorway. More books and grapes are swagged to the sides of the front door with the legends *Inter Folia Fructus*, or "Fruit between the leaves," and *Litera Scripta Manet*, or "What is written lasts." Classifications of knowledge, such as art, philosophy, and literature, are inscribed above the windows.

The classical building is surmounted by a colored terra-cotta frieze showing a continuous design of stylized sphinxes of classical tradition representing learning, knowledge, and erudition. Between the repeated figures, symbols of "great human ideas and mysteries" are placed. The stars represent liberty, the crosses Christianity. Two curved shapes in a circle represent yin and yang or "life formed by male and female elements."[33] The final design, which must have been somewhat of an embarrassment during the late 1930s and 1940s, is a swastika, which was described by Alfred M. Githens in the 1920s as "originating far beyond the beginning of history and common to most of the primitive races of the world, its meaning not always the same, but always beneficent to human beings." Sixty-four stern owls sit on the sills of the second floor windows. Frequently used as symbols for the goddesses of wisdom Minerva or Athena, these wise birds survey Market and King Streets and Rodney Square, protecting the volumes at their backs from fenestral invasion.

The gift of the land, the donations of the 3,000 people who made the new building possible, the high quality of the architects chosen, and their design which goes so far beyond the utilitarian, all testify to local pride. The building received the Medal of Monumental and Government Buildings from the American Institute of Architecture in 1925 for its successful design.[34]

After ten months of use the building was judged to be as successful from the standpoint of administration as of beauty. The staff was able to turn from construction to programs. A hospital service was inaugurated in 1924. Two thousand books were collected, and staff members made weekly hospital and home visits to invalids well enough to read.

The Delawareana program was established with its own mezzanine location and 100 feet of shelves. The ambitious plan was to collect all printed matter relating to the state, including books, pamphlets, articles, and reports of organizations. The materials needed constant cataloguing and classification, but were usable. As the years went on, ever more ambitious plans to codify Delaware material were launched. The acquisition of the 13,000 volume Hilbiber collection, rich in Delawareana, added considerably.[35]

Frederick J. Hilbiber, a Wilmington barber with a shop on Market Street between Fifth and Sixth Streets, was a town character known as a naturalist, minerologist and energetic collecter of old books. Arthur L. Bailey considered Hilbiber's collection as one of the best in the state, and after Hilbiber's death in 1937, Bailey raised funds to purchase the collection.[36]

The ambitious Delawareana collection was so labor intensive

37. Exhibition of the history of the Wilmington Library, April 26 to May 28, 1943.

that in bad times it was the first area to suffer. The cataloging of the backlog of unprocessed books, pamphlets, and broadsides hung over the staff. From time to time special staff was hired to bring the work up to date.

The business and technical department was also established at this time. Several years previously, the library had made a study of the industries of Wilmington and gathered together practical books on each trade and industry. Lists on particular trades were mailed to employees, sometimes enclosed in pay envelopes. This circulation of practical information was a great success. Nields reported in 1923 that five hundred such books circulated each month. Plans were made to upgrade the technical reference collection with donations from industrial firms.

The Lincoln Collection of over 2,000 books, pictures and prints about Abraham Lincoln came to the library as the bequest of Frank G. Tallman with the request that the items be "preserve[d] and exhibit[ed] in an appropriate way." The Lincoln Club of Delaware redecorated a room on the second floor of the library to resemble a period living room to house the collection. The club opened the room, a gift to the library, on Lincoln's birthday and weekly.[37]

The Wilmington Institute Free Library was now at home in a spacious new building, and services were expanding to meet public needs. Board members turned their serious attention to expansion beyond central Wilmington.

SIX

Reaching the People in City and County, 1924 to 1945

I N 1919, THE LIBRARIAN, TWENTY-FOUR ASSISTANTS, AND THREE JANITORS, CATERED TO THE NEEDS OF THE CLIENTS, ATTEMPTING TO ALLOW NO READER OR INQUIRER TO LEAVE THE LIBRARY UNSATISFIED. THE STAFF ENROLLED 20% OF THE LOCAL POPULATION AS CARD HOLDERS AND CIRCULATED 3.8 VOLUMES PER YEAR PER CARD HOLDER. FUNDING FOR THE library amounted to forty-five cents per city resident per year.[1] These figures compared badly with the demanding "reasonable minimum" suggested by the American Library Association, which recommended one dollar per resident to provide community library service. The ALA, which established high standards in an effort to upgrade local institutions, recommended trained librarians, a main library with reading room facilities, branch libraries and reading rooms within easy reach of all the people, registration at 30% of population, expensive reference books, and home use of five volumes per person per year.[2] The library Board could not manage to carry on such services at the rate they were funded. Nevertheless, they planned to expand.

Once the new main building was operating smoothly, the Board of Managers focused attention on increased library services for people at a distance from Rodney Square. Two major plans took shape: the first was to reach the entire County through mobile service, and the second to increase City usage through branch libraries.

The New Castle County Library

Many citizens who lived outside of Wilmington regularly borrowed books from the main building. The expense of their library use was covered by gifts from William Bancroft and not by the regular library budget which depended on city funds. In 1910, 2,672 County

38. A boy scout delivering books, part of the outreach service offered to the community.

borrowers made up about 13% of the library's users. In 1926, 4,043 borrowers accounted for 17%. Countywide use of the facilities continued to grow.

On October 27, 1926, the Board of Managers considered the proposition of Alice P. Smyth to undertake a two year trial of free library work in New Castle County similar to that carried on in New Jersey. Miss Smyth, the library's third major benefactor, offered $12,000 to underwrite the project, requesting that a county librarian be hired, that books be purchased, and that leases for renting "station quarters" be arranged. She asked that the work be a memorial to her friend Mary H. Askew Mather, and was seldom mentioned except as the anonymous donor.[3]

Mary H. Askew Mather had begun New Castle County travelling libraries to rural schools in 1898 under the auspices of the New Century Club of Wilmington. Women's clubs in Maryland, Philadelphia and New Jersey had previously instituted such travelling libraries. Alice Smyth offered funds to extend the service to adults.

The Board gratefully accepted her offer and set to work. The new service was concentrated in small and distant communities in southern New Castle County, and no stations were established in nearby towns which had good trolley service to the main library. On June 30, 1927, stations were established in Bear, Blackbird, Delaware City, Hockessin, Kirkwood, Port Penn, and St. Georges. These stations were only open during brief periods, usually twice a week in the afternoon or evening, in the charge of some local person who served without pay. The next year the library opened more stations in

Corner Ketch, Ogletown, Stanton, Summit Bridge, Townsend, Yorklyn, and Christiana. The New Castle County library system installed small collections of books at each town site and some schools.[4]

The county library network developed rapidly. Nellie Morton, the second director, was a powerful library influence, serving in all for nearly fifty-four years in various capacities. Miss Morton set the county program on its feet. She began in 1928, when there were seventeen stations, and served as director for twenty years. In 1929, there were sixty, nineteen in small communities and forty-one in rural schools. Miss Symth donated an additional $5,000 and a book truck. The New Castle County Levy Court, in response to petitions from 1,400 citizens, passed an act on March 6, 1929, authorizing funds, and appropriating $6,000, "toward the maintenance and support of a free library for the use of the residents of New Castle County outside of the City of Wilmington."[5] The funding of the City and County were closely intertwined, making this complex provision of services even more complex. At least half of the County's revenues came from taxes on property in the City of Wilmington, especially on valuable downtown commercial property.

The New Castle County Free Library, despite its growth and service to a rapidly growing population, remained a small operation

39. An early bookmobile takes the library on the road. Photo by Sanborn Studio, Wilmington.

compared to the Mother institution in the City. In 1932, the City budget and circulation were roughly four times those of the County. The Institute circulated 774,000 volumes and operated on a budget of $86,000, while the County system circulated 178,000 volumes on a budget of $13,000. But while City service was somewhat stabilized, the County service continued to grow, and the next year the book truck made 1,070 visits and covered 13,220 miles. A new book truck was purchased to carry on the work. The County library system operated out of central headquarters in the Wilmington building which served as a base of supplies.[6]

The Country library purchased its own books and established separate collections at each station. When a requested book was not available from the 252 collections administered by the system, the patron had but to ask for the title. In a forerunner of inter-library loan, the request was communicated and filled as promptly as possible from the main collection. The County library system provided incredible personal service, finding the desired volumes and delivering them or sending them out. In 1938, the staff mailed 7,034 books directly to borrowers. In 1942, they mailed 11,450. The County system aimed to

40. A bookmobile in 1933. Photo by Sanborn Studio, Wilmington, Delaware.

provide book services within two miles of every home in the County. Books were also taken directly to the bedsides of shut-in readers throughout the County to supplement the regular hospital service which had begun in 1924. The County library arranged reading courses for teachers, set up story hours, and held meetings for interested groups.[7]

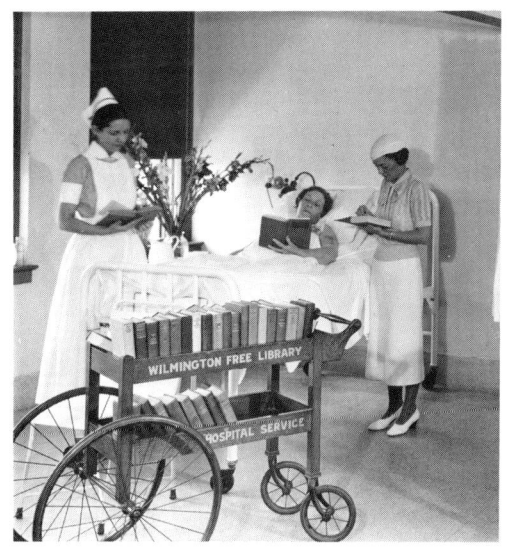

41. A bookmobile services a hospital in 1923, Anna M. Dorsey, librarian.

In the 1940s, the County library had established regular service to forty small communities, fifty-three rural schools, two parochial schools, two private schools, and to ten hospitals and other institutions. The Bookwagon made 1,069 visits to schools and stations and covered 9,520 miles, checking out 180,000 items from the collection of 28,000 books and 8,000 mounted pictures.[8] Circulation was steadily increasing. The County library system pleased everyone by its success and steady growth. The City branches developed more haphazardly.

City Branches

The three small City branches, which had been established around the turn of the century, continued their activity. These three sites were selected almost accidentally because of available space and special circumstances, but they were far from ideal in location and arrangements. The *Rockford Branch*, the first of these small satellites, was established by William Bancroft, the head of Jos. Bancroft & Sons Co., for his employees soon after his contributed funds had made the Wilmington Institute free. The Rockford Branch was taken over by the Library in 1896 and opened May 4, 1897. The small library occupied a large second-story room over a grocery store, about

42. The Woodlawn Branch Library, about 1927, with Emily McGordy and Dorothy Sherwood, librarians.

halfway down the hill on Rockford Road, where it served the mill village community near the Bancroft mills. The library was open three days a week from 3-9 pm in the winter and 6:30-9 pm in the summer.

Jos. Bancroft & Sons Co. furnished the library room, heat, light, and repairs, and donated $500 annually toward costs of about $750. The branch was so isolated that little growth took place. The Rockford Branch was eventually closed on June 30, 1955.[9]

The *Woodlawn Branch*, which was established as a station on the County route in 1908, was made a branch in October of 1925. Located

43. The Talleyville Library Station, about 1924. Sanborn Studio, Wilmington.

at 2201 W. Sixth Street, up a crooked stairway, in a building principally occupied for other purposes, fronting on a quiet street, this little branch was easy to ignore. The library doubled in size in 1926 to comprise two small rooms. This literary corner in the Woodlawn Trustees' administrative building could hold only 1,300 books, although the American Library Association recommended that a branch library have more than 15,000 books. The branch has since moved to 2101 W. Sixth Street.[10]

The *Brandywine Branch* was located in a rent free, City owned, separate building, the Old Brandywine Academy, at 5 Vandever Avenue. Established as a branch in 1915, the library consisted of two small rooms, one above the other, and held 3,600 books in that very limited space. Administration was difficult, and growth in this area was not promising, as the branch was too close to the main library. The Board of Managers suggested the branch be moved or perhaps the space be developed as a children's library.[11]

An additional "library for colored people" was established briefly at No. 22 School in 1921. The bequest of Anne Semple provided funds to make reading materials available, and a collection was purchased and staff assembled. Apparently, the experiment was not successful. The branch was closed, and the funds reverted to the

44. The Belvedere Library Station, about 1950. Sanborn Studio, Wilmington.

Wilmington Institute to be used in other ways to provide books for the black community in accordance with Anne Semple's will.[12]

The Board of Managers recognized an urgent need to extend library services to the neighborhoods. If the library were to grow, as they felt it must, the growth must be, at least in part, through branch libraries. In 1926, the Board engaged Dr. Frank Morton Jones to survey library needs and facilities and make recommendations upon future growth.

Dr. Jones noted that the great majority of main building patrons lived or worked within a one mile radius of the library. Two-thirds of the City of Wilmington was outside that circle. Jones recommended that branches be located about a mile and a half from Rodney Square. He also suggested that the branches should be located so as to call attention to themselves as libraries; they should be attractive and imposing structures rather than rooms hidden up the stairs in some other building. Finally, each branch should be near a line of travel, convenient to public transportation, and noticeable from the road. He recommended four sites for future branches: 30th and Market Streets, Stapler Park or 17th and Bayard Avenue, 2nd and Union Streets, and across the 3rd Street Bridge.[13]

He recommended that the existing three branches, wholly inadequate, should be replaced at once with three new buildings which would cost between $50,000 and $100,000 each. Tilton and Githens, the prize winning architects of the new main library, designed some buildings, considered "altogether admirable." Their four attractive designs were pictured with Jones' report in a handsome brochure, laying out a comprehensive plan for development.[14] The Board members thought that these branches could be built by major benefaction or by popular subscription, and they hoped that the City would maintain them.[15]

45. The Reference Department at 10th and Market Streets in 1936, with Edward Mack, Laussat R. Rodgers, and John Franklin Pote.

The Board distributed the report and took options on two very attractive lots for branch buildings available from the Woodlawn Trustees. But no major benefactors appeared. The options expired on December 20, 1929, during the depression, when there was no hope of erecting any new structures, and the Board decided to take title to the lot at Second and Union Streets and to the lot at Sixteenth and Union Streets anyway, with the understanding that the land would be returned to the Woodlawn Trustees, Inc., if the Library Board decided not to use it for branch libraries. The Board also took title to a site at 29th and Jessup Streets, which was given to the library by the Minquadale Home. The Library paid the cost of improvements for this parcel. These locations were very close to those chosen by Dr.

Frank Morton Jones in his 1926 survey of future library needs of the city.[16]

The building program was cut short by problems in the outside world which nevertheless increased library usage. During the Great Depression, activity at all public libraries grew abnormally. Unemployment increased leisure time, and many out-of-work people read for escape. The library served as a source of education, recreation, and refuge.[17]

The Wilmington Institute felt called on to sustain the morale of the people with a steady supply of useful and entertaining literature. Edith Frank, a librarian during that time, recalled coming in an hour before opening time to put yesterday's returned books back on the empty shelves for the next day's users. When the doors opened, the waiting patrons would rush in and soon every seat would be full. On nice days, borrowers took their books to Rodney Square, hurrying back during outbursts of rain. Actual use of the library peaked in the year 1932-1933, never to be surpassed.

The democratic ideals of the libraries were put to the test during the depression when vagrants and the homeless camped there during the day, bringing their possessions in carts and baby buggies. They

46. Harland A. Carpenter, Director of Library, from 1940 to 1964, presenting a certificate to one of the library's young readers.

used the rest rooms to rinse out their laundry, and read the books and magazines to fill time.

It was with some chagrin that the librarian had to note that circulation decreased as times improved, a trend noted across the nation. He could cheerfully report that the decrease was largely in light fiction, a category furnished, but not always approved, by the librarians. The use of reference books and other serious books increased. Sociology books increased in popularity, as did science. The use of books on industrial arts and fine arts more than doubled as people went back to work. The circulation of history books steadily increased.[18]

Librarians foresaw that adult education should be the chief concern of public libraries. They suggested that patrons be offered a Readers' Advisor to prescribe a course of study complemented with literary and scientific lectures.

The use of children's books also declined in the late thirties. One report, in a tone which was to become increasingly familiar, noted, "The radio, the motion picture and organized sport have captured the child's world, laid hold on his imagination, excited his senses so that he has little time and less patience for the printed word." One child was quoted as saying, "I do not want any more books. Every time I come to the Library I miss Dick Tracy on the radio so I am quitting."[19]

The library began sending fewer books to city school buildings for the home use of students. The program had been in operation in the city since 1902, but as new schools established libraries in their own buildings, this program was less necessary and began to be phased out, finally discontinued in 1940.[20]

A serious nagging need of the library was a retirement plan. Some members of the staff had been employed for over thirty years and needed help for their later years, a problem which the depression threw into clear perspective. By the mid 1930s, seven assistants had begun to contribute from their own salaries to a fund managed by the American Library Association. The Finance Committee raised over nine thousand dollars by private subscription toward annuities for eight members of the staff.[21]

As the United States moved toward World War II, the library experienced major changes. War industries brought many new residents to the area, some of whom had time to register and read books.

The accelerated pace of national defense industries and the intensified and extended program for workers in these industries resulted in broader use of books of science and the useful arts. Public interest in war books grew, and in only two weeks almost fifty readers reserved William L. Shirer's *Berlin Diary*.[22]

Tire and gas rationing cut into library access. Still the library mobilized its resources to help the war effort. The Brandywine Branch closed because necessary repairs to the old Academy could not be undertaken. Shorter hours of service at the central library and the Woodlawn Branch in mid-winter were caused by personnel shortages and oil rationing. Classes in first aid were held, and air raid wardens met in the auditorium. Booklists on "First Aid and Nursing," "Nutrition in Wartime," and "Vegetables for Victory" were printed and distributed. Delaware contributed heavily to the Victory Book Campaign, assembling nationally ten million books for the men in the armed services. Delaware contributed twice her quota with 40,000 volumes.[23]

Circulation was down, and times were troubled. But the war inspired personal and even institutional heroism. When peace returned, it brought renewed life.

SEVEN

Federation,
1945 to 1975

N 1943, HARLAND A. CARPENTER, WHO HAD BECOME THE LIBRARIAN OF THE WILMINGTON INSTITUTE IN 1940, PAUSED TO TAKE NOTE THAT AN IMPORTANT MILESTONE WAS FAST APPROACHING: THE FIFTIETH ANNIVERSARY OF THE OPENING OF THE FREE LIBRARY IN 1894. BACK THEN THE LIBRARY HAD SERVED 70,000 RESIDENTS WITH ALMOST 20,000 VOLUMES. In the fifty years succeeding, and with the advent of the County system, the library served 180,000 people with almost 201,000 books. To celebrate, the staff prepared a documentary exhibition, and John P. Nields, a member of the Board since 1894 and President of the Board of Managers since 1921, compiled a historical sketch which was published.[1] During his term of service, the Institute developed from a small book collection into a large library. He had been largely responsible for the planning and erection of the library building.

After victory in Europe and the Pacific was achieved, a Reader's Assistant program was started to help patrons use the card catalog and give information about services and the location of different parts of the collection. Professional staff members also advised readers about specific books to encourage adult education. The libraries sponsored "Great Books" discussion groups which met year after year.[2]

As emphasis on family life grew after the war, the interest in child training assumed new importance. The reference department compiled a list of "Books for Parents" to distribute. A popular innovation at County headquarters was a shelf for parents and teachers which held copies of each new juvenile book purchased, along with good editions of the standard titles.[3]

Anxious to provide service which would meet the needs of postwar Wilmington, the Board once again considered the recommendations of the American Library Association which suggested that local

47. A discussion of The Great Books, many of which took place in the postwar years.

political jurisdictions should allocate a minimum of $1 per capita annually for public library support for areas with populations of 25,000 and over. Using the population figures of the 1940 census of 69,000 for New Castle County, the per capita income for the County library system was only $.29, far below the $1 per capita the national minimum recommended. The income of the Wilmington Institute Free Library was $91,000, or about $.81 per capita.

What is more, the ALA recommended $1.50 per capita for reasonably good service and $2.00 for superior service. In all cases the Wilmington and New Castle County libraries fell far below the minimum standard of support. The librarian regretted that the two arms of the library would be unable to render service fully adequate to the needs of the people without further support.[4]

The library made its first foray into the technological marvels of the future in 1941, arranging to microfilm the disintegrating pages of the *Every Evening* and the *Journal–Every Evening*. The library also subscribed to the film edition of the *New York Times*. These acquisitions required the purchase of a microfilm reader and a humidity-controlled storage room. The gift of H. Fletcher Brown, a member of the Board, made this progress possible.

The library began in 1943 to circulate a collection of phonograph records. The original group of classical recordings was augmented by children's records and speech recordings. Local musical groups sponsored lectures and concerts of recorded music. The library circulated 14,000 records in 1946, and 25,000 in 1948. An overhead projector and a collection of books on film were contributed by the Wilmington Lions to allow invalids to read books projected on the ceiling.[5]

A major development was the establishment in 1945 of the special Business and Technical Section, long anticipated as a service to business and industry. A number of local industries contributed funds for an experimental three-year program. A subdivision of the Reference Department, the Business and Technical Section included trade catalogs, directories, indices, a vertical file with pamphlets, and subscriptions to thirty-nine additional periodicals. A reference specialist to answer queries was added to the staff.[6] The program expanded rapidly. The assistant in charge presented talks to the public and handled public relations. Thousands of calls for information were answered and logged in.

Library use was up markedly, thanks to the Business and Technical Section and to the circulation of phonograph records. Another contributing factor was use by University of Delaware students from Wilmington who were required to live at home due to a dormi-

48. The Library's first microfilm reader.

tory shortage; they used the library for their assignments.

Looking to the future, the librarian outlined desirable services which should be undertaken as finances became available. A Science, Technology and Business Department should be organized, rather than the current Business and Technical Section which had proved inadequate. Film circulation should follow the successful circulation of records. The branch libraries, so long needed and hoped for, should be constructed. A larger bookmobile should service City areas as well as County areas. The speedy accomplishment of these objectives would place the Wilmington Institute Free Library in the front rank of public libraries serving cities of the size of Wilmington.[7]

The Business and Technical Section was promoted to the status of an independent department of the library in 1951. Brisk service for information on investments, business management and finance, automobile repair, electronics and computers, shorthand education, rockets and missiles, and space exploration was recorded year after year.[8] Clearly this department, with its useful knowledge, was a source of great pride to the staff and Board of Managers.

Reports through the years show a continued bias against fiction. In 1955, when the rate of fiction borrowed dropped to 52% of the books borrowed, still well over half, the staff was proud. One reason frequently given for the declining interest in fiction was that "a generous portion of the new fiction is comprised of psychologically unpleasant situations or characters."[9] The staff also interpreted these statistics as showing the hoped-for shift from reading for diversion to reading for information. Circulation continued to rise despite the advent of television. Requests for books on the ballets, operas, and other productions seen on television increased.

Special services to the children of the city continued. The staff regularly visited the fourth and seventh grades and spoke to groups from various agencies visiting the Children's Room. Staff members also told stories and gave book reviews and talks to many diverse groups.[10]

49. A story hour in the Children's Room, in 1951 when the room was located on the King Street side.

50. A panel discussion on children's books, broadcast on WDEL during Book Week, November 17, 1952. William P. Frank, on the left, was moderator. Sanborn Studio, Wilmington.

Library staff members attempted to meet each request courteously and efficiently, answering many questions a day from patrons in person or on the telephone. But the public face represented a small fraction of the energy expended to keep the library going. Professionally trained librarians selected books to purchase, and then classified and cataloged them. Clerical workers typed catalog cards and filed them. Thousands of books were repaired by book menders. Lists, forms, and publicity releases were processed; and overdue notices and reserve cards were sent to clients. Qualified staff members were needed to perform these tasks, but low salaries precluded filling all available slots with permanent help.[11]

In 1952, the Wilmington Library had forty-six full time personnel, of whom twenty-one were of professional level and twenty-five were assistants or clerks. Additionally there were forty-five people engaged in part-time work or in housekeeping services. The minimum beginning professional salary at that time was $2,800.[12] A national shortage of trained personnel led librarians away from the Wilmington system to others which offered higher salaries, more professional growth, and better working conditions. Strain on the staff increased when school work began to include bibliographic exercises for homework reports. The Reference Room was thronged with high school and college students, filling each chair and sitting on window sills, step ladders, and the floor. The staff added folding chairs and tables, and still could not meet the demand for space. The students called for periodicals and books from the stacks which kept the pages running, and used the microfilm reading machines constantly. The students also put heavy strain on classic works assigned by their teachers. The library bought multiple copies, but the students regularly stripped the shelves. One busy Saturday in March, the librarians counted 2,588 people who came in for service. The staff divided the year between the school-intensive period September to May, and the remaining three and a half summer months when more attention could be paid to the needs of adults, and the collection could be weeded and arranged. This condition continued until the mid-sixties when school library resources improved greatly.[13]

Clearly the shortage of help and the strain on facilities required movement into less labor-intensive operations. The librarians had checked everything in and out by hand. In 1956, after considerable

51. The front of the New Castle County Free Library Branch on Concord Pike, now known as the Concord Pike Library. Photo by Lubitsch & Bungarz.

52. The Lounge of the New Castle County Library, Concord Pike, in 1960.

study and preparation, the circulation department moved into photographic charging.[14]

In 1957, the President of the Board of Managers announced that a headquarters building for the New Castle County Free Library, which the Wilmington Institute had administered since 1927, would be erected through the generous gift of $500,000 from the Longwood Foundation. The Woodlawn Trustees, Inc., for a token payment, sold to the library a tract of land on the Concord Pike near the Alfred I. du Pont School; and the Levy Court of New Castle agreed to provide funds for the operation of the establishment.[15]

Opened April 22, 1959, the Concord Pike facility held administrative and storage spaces, loading platforms for the library's mobile units, and library rooms for adults and children. The use of this new library space immediately exceeded all expectations.

This very successful year also marked the death of Miss Alice P. Smyth whose original grant for the demonstration of County Library service had begun the program. Miss Smyth had continued to donate to the work during her lifetime, and she bequeathed almost $20,000 for an endowment fund for the County service.[16]

County population by 1960 was over 300,000, including 96,000 within the City. While moving the County library to its own facilities freed space in the main building, the urgent need was for greater suburban County facilities. A new mobile library, set on the road in 1961, enabled the County to take its services to thirty-two population centers. But the population still required branch buildings with reading rooms.

By 1962, circulation had climbed to over a million in the combined libraries. 62,000 patrons had registered.[17] The library purchased land on Kirkwood Highway as the site for a building.

The Kirkwood Highway Branch of the New Castle County Free Library was completed and dedicated on March 29, 1967. Built on land acquired from the Catholic Cemeteries of the Diocese of Wilmington, the building was constructed with funds provided by the Levy Court of New Castle County with assistance from the Federal Government under the Library Services and Construction Act. Overwhelming response raised the usage to the level of the Concord Pike Branch almost immediately.[18]

53. The Kirkwood Highway Branch of the New Castle County Free Library completed in 1966, designed by Whiteside, Moeckel and Carbonell.

The expansionist movement continued when the library announced plans to remodel and renovate the main library building at an estimated cost of $1,180,000. The peeling paint, the mosquitoes and other insects entering the unscreened windows, and the endless battle with dirt from the street called out for some treatment. Air conditioning and complete refurbishing would provide the solution to over-crowding, and would extend the useful life of the building, correcting the deficiencies in lighting and space utilization apparent over the years.[19]

Funds were pieced together from the Longwood Foundation, the Library Commission for the State of Delaware, the government of New Castle County, the City of Wilmington, and some private citizens to renovate the building. The aim was to enlarge the capacity of the building and expand services without altering the outward appearance.[20]

While library work continued to grow and develop, the climate of the City was changing. Wilmington suffered considerable strife in the late sixties, and library use reflected the turmoil of the cities. After President Kennedy was assassinated, the library was almost empty of patrons for two days and then closed for a day of national mourning. A six-month bus strike in 1967 cut drastically into circulation. The staff counted all the people entering the Central Library during April 1968. The first Saturday brought 1,107. The following week, after the tragic death of Dr. Martin Luther King, Jr., only 657 people came to the library.[21]

Four days after Dr. King's assassination, which came as the climax of the turbulent civil rights movement, disorder and riots erupted in Wilmington. No mobs attacked the library which had been racially integrated throughout living memory and perhaps always. In a racially segregated culture, when separate schools, movies, restaurants, and buses were the rule, the library provided an enlightened and valuable contrast.

Violent crowds gathered in the streets in 1968, vandalizing stores, setting fires, and thoroughly terrorizing observers, many of whom felt that the City would be destroyed. Wilmington Mayor John Babiarz called on the State for help in quelling the disturbances. Governor Charles L. Terry, Jr. mobilized the entire Delaware Army National

54. The Mobile Library in 1953. Sanborn Studio, Wilmington.

Guard, a force of 3,500, for several days and then, overreacting to what had occurred, kept soldiers on the City streets for nine and a half months.[22] This action, bitterly resented by inner city residents, served to isolate Wilmington from the surrounding area and to make it seem less accessible.

Many were cautious about coming to the center city, and much of the borrowing activity moved to the suburbs. It was, perhaps, a good time to begin the remodeling of the main library.

In July, 1969, the building was stripped of its books, which were moved to temporary quarters across King Street in the former Odd Fellows Building. All operations closed down for one week and then standard service was set up on four levels in the borrowed space. The Business and Technical Department, a separate unit for eighteen years, and the pride of the library, was discontinued and its collection dispersed and intershelved.[23]

The eclectic classically styled library constructed in 1923 and dubbed Roman Imperial by its architects, was extensively redone. The almost fifty-year old building was brought up to date to include a new elevator, new carpeting, book stacks, furniture, and modern heating, cooling, and electrical systems, at a cost of $1,750,000. The classical elements were retained when possible.

55. Christopher B. Devan, Director of Library, inspects plans for remodeling the library, November 17, 1969.

The renovation created three full floors and did away forever with the two-story columns surmounted by the frieze, the wide front staircases, and the central toplighted atrium. The frieze was broken up and lowered to fit between the black columns in sections, rather than sitting on top of them. A mezzanine along the back wall provided book space. Acoustical tile was installed, and the seating and book capacity were doubled. Excellent lighting and accessible shelves were introduced, and the periodicals were relocated to a more convenient place. The general effect, with its columns and frieze, is somewhat similar to the original appearance. Open stacks made many books more accessible to clients. Service was more efficient and improved, but the building lost some of its most attractive and distinguishing features and certainly its original ambiance.

On April 19, 1971, Wilmington celebrated the rededication of the refurbished library. Over 100 guests heard Mr. Charles L. Reese give a brief history of the institution. "Yesterday, we were a city library," he intoned. "Today, we are the headquarters for a county library system reaching nearly four hundred thousand people."[24] The next day 700 citizens attended an Open House, taking home with them 500 borrowed books. Thousands of people thronged the halls the first few weeks, newly impressed by the beautiful building. The Sons of Pericles and Daughters of Athena honored the library for re-installing the Parthenon frieze, "beloved by Wilmingtonians," and for promoting classical heritage.[25]

New services included a paperback book area, head-phones with the phonograph collection, toys for children, and a microfiche reader.

The space of the newly re-modelled main library was twice as large, but the staff was unchanged. This last note has been struck repeatedly through the recent history of the library as financial limitations have caused the steady dwindling of professional librarians and support staff for all areas of operation. The challenge of the modern library has been to continue to increase collections and services while cutting employees. Funding the library was increasingly problematical. Figures indicated that 50% of the Wilmington library users were County residents, and members of the Board of Managers began to meet with City and County officials to devise a plan for coordination and broader funding.[26]

56. The interior of the library during renovation in 1970.

LOOKING FOR THE LIBRARY?
Hop around the corner
to 10th & KING STS.
ODD FELLOWS HALL
& FORMER CHILDREN'S ROOM

57. A billboard advising library patrons of remodeling projects at the temporary home for the library "around the corner."

The New Castle County government had been reorganized in 1967, changing its taxing capabilities. Prior to that time, the County could tax all property in the county, including Wilmington, and spend the funds, in various areas, in the suburbs. The County Government act of 1965 allowed current taxes, but restricted additional taxes on the City by the County for services performed by local municipalities for their residents.[27] Costs for library service for City and for many suburban residents were born by Wilmington funds.

The Wilmington Institute library at this time, which included the New Castle County Library System, consisted of the central building at 10th and Market Streets; the two city branches, Brandywine, which had reopened in 1945 at 2817 Market Street, and Woodlawn at 2106 W. Sixth Street; the Concord Pike Branch Library at 3406 Concord Pike; the Kirkwood Highway Branch at 6000 Kirkwood Highway; and the Mobile library which consisted of two large book trucks; stations with small collections in Arden and Delaware City with 1,805 books; and nine additional locations including community centers, retirement homes, and correctional institutions which together held a total of 2,791 books. Two new mini-libraries at West End Neighborhood House, 815 N. Lincoln St., and Northeast Partners, 2617 N. Claymont Street were established in 1973.[28] These units had grown up to meet the varied and increasing needs of the library's patrons.

Five other public libraries existed in New Castle County which were not related to the Wilmington library system in any way. These libraries had been developed by local initiative, and they provided services which overlapped, and to some extent, duplicated the Wilmington library services. This coexistence called out for cooperation for efficiency and economy.

Complicated support for these many units was parcelled out by the City of Wilmington, other towns and cities, New Castle County, and the Library Commission for the State of Delaware, which also served as the conduit for Federal funds. Besides these agencies, the Wilmington Library received funds from foundations, the business community, and generous individuals, as well as from endowment investments.[29]

The City of Wilmington was financially strapped by the economic stagnation that followed the 1968 disturbances and was eager to have the County assume the responsibility it was bearing for the support of the library. Members of New Castle County Council were eager to improve County libraries. Former Council President Henry Folsom of Newark and Councilman Joseph Toner from the southern part of New Castle County felt that library service outside Wilmington was not adequate, and they favored extending service by having the County assume total responsibility for library service throughout the County, since individual towns were too poor to provide it. And until the County began support of City library services, it could not tax city real estate, including the high-value center city office buildings, above 1967 levels to support a County library system.

Folsom suggested that the New Castle County Council fund county-wide library service through a County per capita tax. The Wilmington Library would be included in the system as the head library. Many favored this proposal in which all County units would be equally managed by a county-wide library board. Wilmington would doubtless have been the star in such a system, which could probably have eventually been extended to include the whole State. But the complex history of the Wilmington Institute, a statutory creation with statutory City funding obligations, could not be dealt with easily.

The Board of Managers of the library resisted absorption by the County. The managers served as a board of trustees of the library with

104

fiduciary obligations of many years' duration which they were unwilling to abandon or change through legislation. They feared the politicization of the library and were not willing to relinquish their voice in managing the institution. They also feared loss of control over the hiring of staff members and the possible dictation of choice of books and use of funding. They were certainly not willing to give up control without a commitment that the Wilmington Library would get its fair share of funding.

Continuous discussions during the 1972-1974 period led to a "federated" County library system consisting of County owned and operated public libraries and private libraries operating under contractual affiliation agreements intended to provide for coordinated service and County funding. The Wilmington Library proposed the federated system which was adopted. The Wilmington Library maintained its individual identity, and the Board of Managers retained control of the library with the efficiency of County processing of

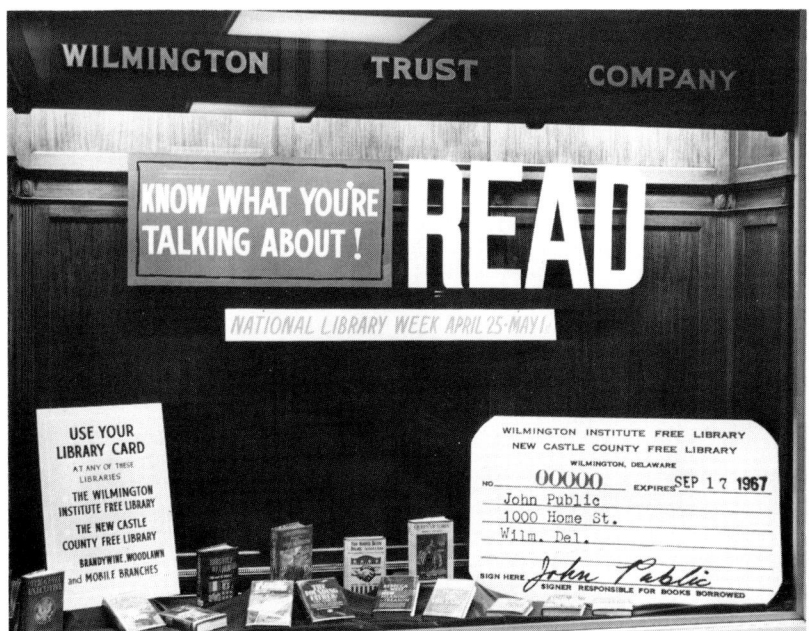

58. National Library Week display at the Wilmington Trust Company, April 25 to May 1, 1965. Lubitsch & Bungarz, Wilmington.

books and a guarantee of support funds.

This major decision came at a time when the library suffered from a serious internal problem. The director, Jack Bryant, was accused of misappropriating over $75,000 of library funds which he used to buy 250 pieces of oriental porcelain for his personal collection. Tried and convicted of this felony, Bryant, who had authored the federated plan, left the institution summarily. He served a year in prison of a five year sentence before he was paroled. The porcelain collection was sold to recoup library funds.[30]

The federated plan preserved the identity of the venerable library which could well have been lost at this juncture. The easy action would have been to accept County control and funds because of the City's straitened condition. In that case, the library would have moved to a homogeneous level with the other institutions in the system, largely losing the historic and cultural differences which set it apart. Once relinquished, the independence of the institution could not have been regained. It can, of course, be argued that the Wilmington Library might have fared better had it become an enthusiastic member of the new system.

On July 1, 1975, the New Castle County Library Department was established. The County then processed the books for Wilmington and for the two City branches, Woodlawn and Brandywine, as well as the County libraries. Concord Pike and Kirkwood Highway Branches, which had been part of the Wilmington Library, entered the County system as regular members. The Wilmington Library director continued to be appointed by the Board of Managers of the Wilmington Library which remained a private entity, affiliated to the County system.[31]

EIGHT

The Information Place, 1975 to 1988

THE MODERN LIBRARY EMBODIES THE WIDELY HELD IDEA THAT EVERYONE, REGARDLESS OF BIRTH OR POSITION, MUST BE EDUCATED TO BE A WORTHY CITIZEN. FREE PUBLIC LIBRARIES STAND BESIDE FREE PUBLIC SCHOOLS IN THIS EDUCATIONAL PROCESS, PROVIDING ENRICHMENT AND FURTHER OPPORTUNITIES FOR THOSE WHOSE FORMAL SCHOOLING HAS ended. Today's libraries aim to broaden readers' interests, to help them with vocational problems, and to supply good recreational reading. Every effort is made to attract all classes of people, to remove all hindrances, to make the widest possible use of books and other materials. The library aims to be the people's university and is willing to be the people's entertainment.

A public library system requires money, vision, local pride, a belief in education, and the feeling that literacy will strengthen democracy and enhance morality. Idealists defend libraries for bringing culture and virtue to the masses. Detractors argue that libraries pander to popular tastes.

Today's Wilmington Library bears little resemblance to the little club which mutually owned a shelf of high-toned books two hundred years ago. Information now comes packaged in videos, computerized data bases, tapes, and micro-formats, as well as bound volumes. Exhibitions, workshops, and discussions augment solitary reading. Libraries utilize the formats of advertising and participatory education to promote knowledge and learning and to sell their services to the public. These once staid institutions now openly compete with popular entertainment for the patrons' leisure hours.

A vast array of new programs blossomed in the Wilmington Library in the period immediately after the federated New Castle County system went into effect. Children's programming increased to include theatre presentations, concerts, films, and puppet shows, as well as safety, health, and animal programs. Library tours and story hours continued. Programming for young adults offered workshops on photography and creative writing along with other educational seminars. Program specialists offered classes on such adult interests as kite building, bee-keeping, needlework, investment management, flower arrangement, and tax information. Adults and children sampled many sources of information besides the books traditionally available.

Bad times brought severe limitations to special programming. The Wilmington Library had proposed the concept of contractual affiliation, adopted in early 1974, which retained the library's private status while accepting the idea of County funding. But while the County had accepted responsibility for the Wilmington Library's financial support, specific funding agreements were never tied down to a contract. As no minimal level of support was ever established, most of the additional revenue was diverted to county-wide use. The very first budget, following the new contractual arrangement, was a disappointment.

Returning to the old system of support was not possible. Even if Wilmington were to resume support for the library, City property would not be excluded from the burden of double taxation for library service. When the late 70s brought ruinous inflation, and book prices and other costs doubled, the Wilmington Library experienced a relative decline in County support.[1]

59. The Circulation Department at 10th and Markets Streets, as seen from the mezzanine. Photo, Wade Lawrence.

Collections suffered. Due to a shrinking income and rising costs, the number of books purchased decreased. Librarians pointed out that a 10% annual increase in the number of books was necessary to keep the collection current and circulation growing. When the number of new books dipped below that figure, the borrowing figures went down. For several years in a row, the collection actually decreased as more worn-out books were weeded out of the system than new ones were added.

The staff shrank. In 1976, forty-four full time personnel administered the library. Four years later, only twenty-six were still employed. The ambitious programming developed only a few years previously had to be abandoned. All non-essential programs were put on hold while the remaining staff struggled to maintain basic and essential services. "Collection Management," that labor intensive effort needed to maintain an inventory of books, was overwhelming.[2]

60. Christoffer Taxell, Finnish Minister of Education, presents a gift of books to Willard A. Speakman, Chairman of the Board of Managers on April 14, 1988. Bungarz Foto.

Subtle changes in the Wilmington Library's leadership role were noted. Wilmington was the senior library, and since 1965, had served as the resource center for all public libraries in the state. In 1968, when the University of Delaware began a teletype service for Interlibrary Loan Services, the two programs overlapped for a year and a half in "uneasy co-operation." The University's program DRILL, Delaware Rapid Inter Library Loan, prevailed. When the position of State Librarian was filled, DRILL, the Statewide program, was centered there. After the New Castle County library consolidation, the County took on the

61. William F. Renzulli, Wilmington artist, autographs his poster of the Wilmington Library. Photo by Sam Trasatti.

responsibility of processing books for all County library units. The Wilmington Library's state-wide influence diminished as other institutions grew.[3]

In 1981, Willard A. Speakman, President of the Library's Board of Directors, appointed a Strategic Planning Team to consider long range objectives to help the library maintain a stable foundation while being thrown, headlong, into the future. The Board asked the team to survey the community to determine needs, and to plan an integrated automated library system. Identifying community businessmen as major users, the group named a committee to plan a new business and technical library.[4]

The staff moved into the computer age in the early 80s to blend traditional library services with forward looking systems and services. "The Information Place" function needed to be improved, but the community library had to be maintained. Mechanical brains partially

PLACE TO REMEMBER

1788-1988

WILMINGTON LIBRARY

compensated for the loss of staff. In 1979, the Library, with the assistance of federal funds and in cooperation with the State Library, automated its cataloging and out-of-state inter-library loan system. The system automated book purchasing and processing in 1981, office administration in 1983, and database searching at the reference desk in 1984.

The Library had been involved with film for a long time. Noon-time and Sunday programs, calling attention to new library acquisitions and encouraging the circulation of films for home use, began in 1975. The statewide free film borrowing program began in 1978 and grew tremendously. In 1984 the Library began to charge a fee for the rental of films, and expanded service to include the popular and more portable audio and video cassettes.

Dr. Guy Garrison, Dean of the College of Information Studies at Drexel University, was commissioned in 1984 to study the future of the Library within the federated system of libraries in New Castle County. The report concluded that the level of library funding was

62. A patron selects a video cassette for rental with help from staff members Pamela Messick and Deborah Howard. The Audio Visual Center, on the King Street level, occupies the original space of the Children's Room. Photo by Sam Trasatti.

63. Access to the King Street level for handicapped patrons was made available in November of 1987.

not adequate for the type of multipurpose central library one would expect in Wilmington, and laid out several bleak alternatives. The Board decided to seek additional funding rather than to cut services. The library would continue the contract with New Castle County, and with the anticipated additional funding, would upgrade current levels of service and collections, increase the staff, and plan and carry out long range future growth. A five year plan outlined the future mission of the Library. It would continue to provide a mix of services both as a community library for inner city and suburban daily patrons, and as a major resource center providing increasing informational and research services. The bywords of the plan were Availability—increasing collections and services with State funds, endowments, and grants; Accessibility—relocating collections to encourage greater access; Administrative Control—using computer services; and Community Awareness—increasing public relations and programing.[5]

The main library continued to service three satellites: the Woodlawn and Brandywine Branches and La Biblioteca del Pueblo, a Spanish-English library branch which joined the Library in 1979. Started in 1972 as an outreach program at St. Paul's Church, La Biblioteca moved in 1976 to 4th and Harrison Streets and later back to the Church for more space. La Biblioteca, originally supported by federal funds, was supported by the County after 1984. The bi-lingual library moved in 1987 to its present location, a row house at 1129 W. 4th Street. There, a collection of 3,000 books along with Spanish language records, magazines, and books formed a focal point for a lively community center.[6]

Another positive development was the founding of the Friends of the Library in 1978. Wilmingtonians, who had long loved the Library, organized to help it in these difficult years. The Friends aimed to increase the visibility of library services and to raise funds for desirable projects. The growing power and support of the Friends brought in $12,000 for books and equipment in 1986 and nearly $20,000 in 1987,[7] via food festivals, antique shows, and volunteer coordination. Since 1987, the Friends have maintained an attractive book shop on the main floor where duplicate and donated books can be purchased at a fraction of the list price. Female leaders of the Friends have been named to the Board of Managers since the group's inception.

On November 10, 1983 the Wilmington Library's Literacy Program was established. As an affiliate of the Literacy Volunteers of America, the Library trained volunteer tutors to help raise the reading abilities of adult students to at least fifth grade level. The

64. Tutor and pupil work on reading in connection with the Literacy Volunteers of America. Photo by Sam Trasatti.

65. Children and balloons were part of the celebration of the library's 200th anniversary during a popular Family Night Open House in 1988.

Literacy Program, part of the national movement, exemplified the idealistic way a library could assist the community to further adult education. From the beginning, the program was funded by grants and private contributions. By the end of 1987, nearly 200 volunteers were teaching reading.[8]

The Library continued to experiment to improve services. The Friends assisted with staffing the public service desks. Read Aloud Delaware, a group formed to encourage mothers to read to their children, began to work with the Children's Department. A reading incentive program attracted growing numbers of elementary school students.

In 1984, the General Assembly increased aid to libraries, raising the level of support from $.13 to $.39 per capita, affording assistance to all libraries in the State including $40,000 to the Wilmington Library. This boon, along with additional County funds, continued long range planning, efforts for library automation, implementation of fee-based services, and growing "grass-roots" support, promised a brighter future for the struggling library.[9]

116

During the expansion boom of the early 80s, some officials of the City administration proposed selling the very valuable City-owned land on which the library stands and erecting a modern library building elsewhere. But they had failed to consider the deep affection of the public for the institution and the building itself. A public outcry caused the City to reject the concept of relocation. For now, at least, the library will stay on Rodney Square where it has been for over sixty-five years.

The Library building, extensively remodelled in 1969, underwent additional improvements when steam and chilled water were introduced from the DuPont building at 10th and Market Streets for heating and cooling purposes in 1986. The stately Roman matron of Rodney Square was refurbished and refaced in preparation for her 200th anniversary of continuous service. A new roof, interior and exterior painting, and lighting repairs added to public awareness that something momentous was about to occur. In 1988, the Library mounted a major fund raising campaign.

The Wilmington Library has endured for two hundred years, in good times and in bad. With public support, this majestic edifice, and the enlightening collections within, should continue to provide a vital community service for another two hundred years.

Notes

Chapter 1

1. Receipt for dues, Collection of the Wilmington Library, hereafter cited as WL.
2. A.T. Lincoln, *Wilmington, Delaware: Three Centuries Under Three Flags* (Rutland, Vermont, c. 1937), 107.
3. Richard L. Bushman and Anna L. Hawley, *A Random Sample of Kent County, Delaware, Estate Inventories, 1727-1775* (Newark, Delaware, 1987).
4. Benjamin Franklin, *The Autobiography of Benjamin Franklin* (New York, 1962), 71-72.
5. Jesse H. Shera, *Foundations of the Public Library: The Origins of the Public Library Movement in New England, 1629-1955* (Chicago, 1949), 55.

Chapter 2

1. Harold B. Hancock, *Delaware Two Hundred Years Ago: 1780-1800 (Wilmington, 1987)*, 57.
2. "Minute Book of Wilmington Library Company from 1787 to 1818," WL.
3. Hancock, *Delaware Two Hundred Years Ago*, 173.
4. Richard L. Mumford and Rodney F. Allen, "The New Castle Library Company: The Founding and Early History of a Subscription Library, 1811-1850," *Delaware History*, 11(1965)282- 295.
5. "Minute Book of the Wilmington Library," 7 July 1794.
6. John P. Nields, *The Wilmington Public Library and The New Castle County Free Library: A Historical Sketch* (Wilmington, 1943), 6, 7.
7. "Minute Book of the Wilmington Library," 11 February 1816.
8. Nields, *A Historical Sketch*, 9; "Minutes of the Wilmington Library," 7 March, 4 April 1818.7.
9. The correct title of this book is *Address to the Government of the United States* by Charles Brockden Brown, well known journalist and novelist, published in 1803.
10. "Minute Book of the Wilmington Library."
11. Linda Bove McKinstry, "Delaware Learned Societies: 1785-1893," (unpublished M.A. thesis, University of Delaware, 1985), 21, 22.
12. David Kaser, *A Book for Sixpence: The Circulating Library in America* (Pittsburgh, 1980), 11.

13. *Ibid.*, 12.
14. Evald Rink, *Printing in Delaware, 1761-1800,* (Wilmington, Delaware, 1969), provides an invaluable listing of books published in Delaware.
15. Jesse H. Shera, *Foundations of the Public Library: The Origins of the Public Library Movement in New England, 1629-1855* (Chicago, 1949), 55, 69.
16. Kaser, *A Book for Sixpence,* 60.
17. This movement is discussed at length in Devendra P. Varma, *The Evergreen Tree of Diabolical Knowledge* (Washington, D.C., 1972). Varma quotes "The Use of Circulating Libraries," published in 1797 which suggests a 1,500 volume collection, of which 70% was to be fiction, p. 198.
18. Kaser, *A Book for Sixpence,* 8-9, 32-33, 41.
19. Shera, *Foundations of the Public Library,* 139.
20. Elmer D. Johnson, *History of Libraries in the Western World,* a revised version of Michael H. Harris, *Histories of Libraries in the Western World* (Metuchen, N.J., 1970), 175, 176.
21. Harold B. Hancock, *Delaware Two Hundred Years Ago: 1780- 1800* (Wilmington, Delaware, 1987), 173-184.
22. Robert A. Gross, "Much Instruction from Little Reading: Books and Libraries in Thoreau's Concord," *Proceedings of the American Antiquarian Society,* 97 (Part 1, 1987), 157.
23. *Ibid.*, 152-53.
24. Shera, Foundations of the Public Library, 103.
25. Edwin Wolf, 2nd., "Franklin and His Friends Choose Their Books," in John David Marshall, ed. *An American Library History Reader: Contributions to Library Literature* (Hamden, Connecticut, 1961), 20-21.
26. Kaser, *A Book for Sixpence,* 88, illustrates the increasing numbers of American novels published: 28 in the years between 1810 and 1819, 765 between 1840 and 1849, 2,933 between 1850 and 1875, and 6,175 between 1875 and 1900; 89.
27. *Ibid.*, 116, 118, 121, 126.

Chapter 3

1. "Minutes of the Wilmington Library," 27 April, 4 May 1850.
2. *Ibid*, 3 January, 7 March, 2 May, 1846.
3. McKinstry, "Delaware Learned Societies," 41.
4. "Proceedings of the Young Men's Association and the Executive Committee Thereof, Commencing 1855," 7 April 1856, WL.
5. Nields, *A Historical Sketch,* 13, 14; "Minutes of the Wilmington Library," 3 May, 13 September 1856.
6. "Proceedings of the Young Men's Association," 1 December 1857.
7. Nields, *A Historical Sketch,* 10-12, 27; "Proceedings of the Young Men's Association," 5, 15 December 1857.
8. *A Historical Sketch of the Wilmington Library, and Young Men's Association, with the Constitution, By-Laws, &C., and a List of Officers & Members* (Wilmington, 1858); Nields, *A Historical Sketch,* 16.
9. William S. Hilles, Esq., *Annual Report of the Wilmington Institute, 1862.* Hereafter annual reports of the institution will be cited as *Report* with date.

10. Johnson, *History of Libraries in the Western World*, 171-176.
11. Sidney Ditzion, "Mechanics and Mercantile Libraries," *Library Quarterly*, 10(1940), 200.
12. Frances Moltenberry, "History of Peabody Institute Library: University of the People," in John David Marshall, ed., *Approaches to Library History: Proceedings of the Second Library History Seminar, Florida State University Library School, Tallahassee, March 4, 5, and 6, 1965* (Tallahassee, 1966), 152.
13. Ditzion, "Mechanics and Mercantile Libraries," 197-201.
14. *Report, 1888.*
15. "Minutes of the Wilmington Institute, 1862-1866," 12, 26 March 1861.
16. Lincoln, *Wilmington, Delaware*, 108.
17. "Minutes of the Wilmington Institute," 18 December 1860.
18. *Ibid.*, 29 January 1861.
19. Report, 1961.
20. The building was later remodelled to have a Market Street entrance, up two stairs. Patrons of the library in its later days remember the building in this way.
21. "Minutes of the Wilmington Institute," 15 April 1862.
22. *Ibid.*, 4 June 1867, 14 September 1869, 22 February 1870.
23. *Ibid.*, 16 April 1864.
24. Report, 1862.
25. Report, 1864.
26. "Minutes of the Wilmington Institute," 22 May, 25 September, 1866; 10 September 1867; 4 February, 1868.
27. *Ibid.*, 22 February 1890, 3 Jauary 1871, 16 April 1867.
28. *Ibid.*, 16 February 1864, 23 February 1864.
29. *Ibid.*, 10 March 1863.
30. *Ibid.*, 7 October 1862, 6 April, 27 October, 3 November 1863; Report, 1864.
31. "Minutes of the Wilmington Institute," 7 May, 30 April 1861; Report, 1862.
32. "Minutes of the Wilmington Institute," 1 September 1862, 3 February 1863.
33. *Ibid.*, 3 April 1865.
34. *Ibid.*, 23 May 1865; Report, 1865.
35. Carol E Hoffecker, Wilmington, Delaware: *Portrait of an Industrial City, 1830-1910* (Charlottesville, Virginia, 1974), 101.
36. "Minutes of the Wilmington Institute," 6 April 1868, *Report, 1868.*
37. "Minutes of the Wilmington Institute," 9 April, 9 July, 20 August 1867; *Report, 1868.*
38. "Minutes of the Wilmington Institute," 30 April 1869; *Report, 1870.*
39. "Minutes of the Wilmington Institute," 5 April, 14 December 1869.
40. *Report, 1868.*
41. "Minutes of the Wilmington Institute," 11 February, 24 March 1868; *Report, 1868*
42. "Minutes of the Wilmington Institute," 11 June 1862, 6 May 1873; *Report, 1881.*
43. *Report, 1862; Report, 1883; Report, 1885.*
44. *Report, 1887*; Hoffecker, *Portrait of an Industrial City*, 156.
45. *Report, 1888; Report, 1894-1895.*
46. *Report, 1871; Report, 1874; Report, 1884; Report, 1887.*
47. W.S. Auchincloss in *Report, 1877.*
48. *Report, 1887; Report, 1888.*
49. In 1863, membership was 666, volumes 6,000, circulation 18,000. In 1888, the numbers in those same categories were 663, 16,484, and 33,119, *Report, 1888.*

Chapter 4

1. *Report,* 1877.
2. Johnson, *History of Libraries in the Western World,* 230.
3. Shera, *Foundations of the Public Library,* 192, 198.
4. Shera, *Foundations of the Public Library,* 214-15.
5. *Report,* 1892, for instance.
6. *Exercises at the Opening of the New Building of The Wilmington Institute Free Library, Wilmington, Delaware, May Fifth,* 1923, 8-9.
7. *Report,* 1894-1895.
8. Nields, *A Historical Sketch,* 9.
9. "Minutes of the Wilmington Institute," 9 December 1893; *Report,* 1894-1895.
10. *Report,* 1908-1909.
11. *Report,* 1895-1896; *Report,* 1896-1897.
12. *Report,* 1899.
13. *Report,* 1981.
14. *Report,* 1902-03, *Report,* 1906-07.
15. *Report,* 1905-06.
16. *Report,* 1912-1913, *Report,* 1913-1914.
17. *Report,* 1905-06, *Report,* 1907-08, *Report,* 1910-11.
18. *Report,* 1903-04; *Report* 1906-07.
19. *Report,* 1935-36.
20. *Report,* 1906-07.
21. *Report,* 1907-08.
22. *Report,* 1913-14; *Report,* 1914-15.
23. *Report,* 1906-07; *Report,* 1907-08; *Report,* 1908-09.
24. *Report,* 1911-12; *Report,* 1912-13.
25. *Report,* 1910-11; *Report,* 1915-16.
26. *Report,* 1905-06; *Report,* 1910-11; *Report,* 1913-14.
27. *Report,* 1904-05; *Report* 1905-06; *Report,* 1907-08; *Report,* 1909-10.
28. *Report,* 1912-13; *Report,* 1913-14; *Report,* 1914-15; *Report,* 1915-16.
29. *Report,* 1894-95; *Report,* 1910-11.
30. *Report,* 1911-12; *Report,* 1913-14; *Report,* 1914-15.
31. *Report,* 1913-14.

Chapter 5

1. *Report,* 1914-15; Lincoln, *Wilmington, Delaware,* 110.
2. *Report,* 1913-14; *Report,* 1914-15.
3. "Resolution WIFL"; Arthur L. Bailey to J.J. Raskob, 7 April 1913, John J. Raskob Collection, Hagley Museum and Library, hereafter cited as HML..
4. Marjorie McNinch, "The Changing Face of Rodney Square," *Delaware History,* 21(Spring-Summer 1985)3, *passim.*
5. *Ibid.,* 147.
6. "Memoranda in Re Library Site," 3 May 1915, Raskob Papers, HML.
7. J.J. Raskob to William Bancroft, 10 April 1913, Raskob Papers, HML.

8. "Resolution" n.d., Raskob Papers, HML.
9. Purchase agreement, 17 July 1919; John P. Nields to William S. Hilles, Esq. 31 May 1919; in "Library, Sale of Property," file #6872, HML.
10. Pierre S. du Pont to John P. Nields, 22 September 1915; John P. Nields to Pierre S. du Pont, 8 December 1914, Pierre S. du Pont Collection, HML.
11. Pierre S. du Pont to John P. Nields, 21 March 1916, HML.
12. Exercises at the Opening, 10.
13. Report, 1916-17.
14. "A New Library Building," 1916, Pierre S. du Pont papers, HML.
15. "Wilmington Institute Fund for Removal of Graves," 27 July 1917, Pierre S. du Pont papers, HML.
16. Report, 1917-18; Report, 1918-19.
17. Report, 1918-19.
18. Undated flyer, c. 1917, italics his, Raskob papers, HML.
19. Report, 1916-17.
20. Report, 1917-18.
21. John P. Nields to Pierre S. du Pont, 7 April 1921, HML.
22. "Library Notes," 1921, #687, Pierre S. du Pont papers, HML.
23. Report, 1920-21, Ordinance passed 12 May 1921, approved by mayor on 29 May 1921.
24. John P. Nields to Pierre S. du Pont, 13 May 1921, HML.
25. Report, 1920-21; Report, 1921-22.
26. Nields, A Historical Sketch, 11; Report, 1922-23; Lincoln, Wilmington, Delaware, 112.
27. Tilton & Githens to Edgar M. Hoopes, Jr., Esc., 22 December 1921, Raskob papers, HML.
28. Report, 1923-24.
29. Exercises at the Opening of the New Building, 10, 11.
30. Edward L. Tilton and Alfred Morten Githens, "The Wilmington Public Library: Its Inception and Development," Architecture 48(July 1923)1, 218.
31. Tilton and Githens, "The Wilmington Public Library," 213.
32. Quoted in Nields, A Historical Sketch, 14. Letter in possession of the Wilmington Library.
33. Ibid.
34. Report, 1924-25.
35. Report, 1918-19; Report, 1923-24.
36. A.O.H. Grier, This Was Wilmington (Wilmington, Delaware, 1945), 216.
37. Report, 1938-39; Report, 1940-41; Report, 1960-61.

Chapter 6

1. Report, 1919.
2. Report, 1922.
3. Richard L. Mumford and Rodney F. Allen, "The New Castle Library Company: The Founding and Early History of a Subscription Library, 1811-1850," Delaware History 11(1965)282- 295.
4. Report, 1927-28; Nields, A Historical Sketch, 15, 16.
5. Report, 1927-28; Report, 1929-30.

6. *Report, 1931-32; Report, 1932-33.*
7. *Report, 1933-34.*
8. *Report, 1942-43.*
9 *Report, 1954-55.*
10 *Report, 1925-26; Report, 1927-28;* Frank Morton Jones, *Library Service for "Greater Wilmington,"* A report on the present service and future expansion of the Wilmington Institute Free Library (Wilmington, 1926), 11-15.
11. Jones, *Library Service,* 15-18.
12. *Report, 1921-22; Report, 1927-28.*
13. *Report, 1925-26.*
14. *Report, 1926-27;* "Branch Libraries for Wilmington," 1927, Raskob Papers, HML.
15. *Report, 1928-29.*
16. *Report, 1931-32; Report, 1932-33; Report, 1933-34.*
17. *Report, 1930-31.*
18. *Report, 1933-34; Report, 1935-36.*
19. *Report, 1935-36; Report, 1938-39.*
20. *Report, 1935-36; Report, 1939-40*
21. *Report, 1933-34; Report, 1937-38*
22. *Report, 1940-41.*
23. *Report, 1941-42; Report, 1942-43*

Chapter 7

1. John P. Nields, *The Wilmington Public Library and The New Castle County Free Library: A Historical Sketch* (Wilmington, 1943). In his brief history, Judge Nields regrets that he was unable to find many early references to the library which he finds quoted elsewhere. Perhaps he was not able to locate the early minute books in the library's collection which contain the information he refers to. *Report, 1942-43.*
2. *Report, 1947-48; .Report, 1948-49*
3. *Report, 1941-42.*
4. *Report, 1944-45.*
5. *Report, 1943-44; Report, 1944-45; Report, 1945-46;Report, 1947-48.*
6. *Report, 1945-46.*
7. *Report, 1946-47.*
8. *Report, 1950-51; Report, 1961-62.*
9. *Report, 1954-55; Report, 1963-64.*
10. *Report, 1949-50.*
11. *Report, 1951-52.*
12. Esther L. Height, "Survey Report, The Wilmington Institute Free Library with emphasis on The Children's Room," (unpublished M.S. thesis, Columbia University, 1952), 12, 14.
13. *Report, 1957-58; Report, 1963-64.*
14. *Report, 1955-56.*
15. *Report, 1956-57.*
16. *Report, 1958-59.*
17. *Report, 1960-61; Report, 1962-63.*
18. *Report, 1966-67.*

19. *Report,* 1964-65; *Report,* 1965-66; *Report,* 1966-67.
20. *Report,* 1967-68.
21. *Report,* 1963-64; *Report,* 1966-67; *Report,* 1967-68.
22. *News Journal* (Wilmington), 4 April 1988, Dl.
23. *Report,* 1969-70
24. *Report,* 1971-72.
25. *Report,* 1971-72.
26. *Report,* 1972-73.
27. "The government of New Castle County . . . shall not impose an *ad valorem* tax on property within any municipality to pay the cost of any local service function if such function is performed by the municipality for its residents and the cost thereof is paid out of municipal revenue." [Title 9, Section 1157(e); revenues at the 1965 rate were excluded by section 1160.]
28. *Report,* 1970-71; *Report,* 1973-74.
29. *Report,* 1967-68.
30. *Every Evening* (Wilmington, Delaware), 7 May, 2 December 1976.
30. *Report,* 1986.

Chapter 8

1. Richard Abrams, "Summary of the Transfer, History and Status of Wilmington Institute Public Funding Support Obligations of New Castle County," WL.
2. *Report,* 1981-82; *Report,* 1982-83.
3. *Report,* 1970-71; *Report,* 1977-78.
4. *Report,* 1982-83; *Report,* 1983-84.
5. *Report,* 1985-86.
6. *Report,* 1983-84.
7. *Report,* 1986-87; *Report,* 1987-88.
8. *Report,* 1987-88.
9. *Report,* 1983-84.

Bibliography

Books

Davis, Richard Beale. *A Colonial Southern Bookshelf: Reading in the 18th Century*. Athens, Georgia: University of Georgia Press, 1979.

Eaton, Thelma, ed. *Contributions to American Library History*. Champaign, Illinois: The Illini Union Bookstore, 1961.

Franklin, Benjamin. *The Autobiography of Benjamin Franklin*. With a New Introduction by Lewis Leary. New York: Macmillan Publishing Co., Inc., 1962.

Grier, A. O. H., *This Was Wilmington*. Wilmington, Delaware: News Journal Co., 1945

Hancock, Harold B. *Delaware Two Hundred Years Ago: 1780-1800*. Wilmington, Delaware: The Middle Atlantic Press, 1987.

Hessel, Alfred. *A History of Libraries*. Translated, with supplementary material, by Reuben Peiss. Washington, D. C.: Scarecrow Press, 1950.

Hoffecker, Carol. *Corporate Capital: Wilmington in the Twentieth Century*. Philadelphia: Temple University Press, 1983.

_____. *Wilmington, Delaware: Portrait of an Industrial City, 1830-1910*. Charlottesville: Published for the Eleutherian Mills-Hagley Foundation by the University Press of Virginia, 1974.

Johnson, Elmer D. *History of Libraries in the Western World*. Metuchen, N.J.: The Scarecrow Press, Inc., 1970. Second Edition, revised by Michael H. Harris, *History of Libraries in the Western World*. Metuchen, N.J.: The Scarecrow Press, Inc., 1984.

Kaser, David. *A Book for Sixpence: The Circulating Library in America*. Pittsburgh, Pennsylvania: Beta Phi Mu, 1980.

Lincoln, A. T. *Wilmington, Delaware: Three Centuries Under Three Flags*. Rutland, Vermont: The Tuttle Publishing Co., Inc., c. 1937.

Public Libraries in the United States of America: Their History, Condition, and Management. A Special Report. Washington, D. C.: Department of the Interior, Bureau of Education, 1876.

Rink, Evald. *Printing in Delaware, 1761-1800.* Wilmington, Delaware: Eleutherian Mills Historical Library, 1969.

Shera, Jesse H. *Foundations of the Public Library: The Origins of the Public Library Movement in New England, 1629-1855.* Chicago: The University of Chicago Press, 1949.

Varma, Devendra P. *The Evergreen Tree of Diabolical Knowledge.* Washington, D. C.: Consortium Press, 1972.

Articles

Bailey, Arthur L. "The Business Man and the Library." *Equitable Trust Company Monthly.* Volume 5, No. 2, September 1924, pp. 1-4.

Baumgartner, Barbara Walker. "The New Castle County Free Library, 1927-1933." *Delaware History.* XIII(April, 1968)46-56.

Ditzion, Sidney. "Mechanics and Mercantile Libraries." *Library Quarterly.* Volume 10, 1940, pp. 192-219.

Gross, Robert A. "Much Instruction from Little Reading: Books and Libraries in Thoreau's Concord." *Proceedings of the American Antiquarian Society.* Volume 97, Part 1, 1987, 129-188. From Semiannual Meeting, Boston, April 15, 1987.

Harland, J. F., editor and publisher. "The Wilmington Institute Free Library." *The Mediator: Dedicated to the Port of Wilmington, Delaware.* Volume 3, No. 2, 1923, p. 42.

Hoffecker, Carol. "19th Century Wilmington: Satellite or Independent City?" Delaware History. 15(April 1972)1, 1-18.

Korty, Margaret B. "Benjamin Franklin and Eighteenth Century American Libraries." *Transactions of the American Philosophical Society.* New Series, 55(1965).

McNinch, Marjorie. "The Changing Face of Rodney Square." *Delaware History.* 21(Spring-Summer 1985)3, 139-163.

Moltenberry, Frances. "History of Peabody Institute Library: University of the People." John David Marshall, ed. *Approaches to Library History: Proceedings of the Second Library History Seminar, Florida State University Library School, Tallahassee, March 4, 5, and 6, 1965.* Tallahassee, Florida: Journal of Library History, 1966, pp. 151-164.

Mumford, Richard L. and Rodney F. Allen. "The New Castle Library Company: The Founding and Early History of A Subscription Library, 1811-1850." *Delaware History.* 11(1965)282-295.

Tilton, Edward L. and Alfred Morten Githens. "The Wilmington Public Library: Its Inception and Development." *Architecture.* Volume 48, No. 1, July 1923, pp. 213-223.

Wolf, Edwin, 2nd. "Franklin and His Friends Choose Their Books." John David Marshall, ed. *An American Library History Reader: Contributions to Library Literature.* Hamden, Connecticut: The Shoe String Press, Inc., 1961, pp. 17-44.

Pamphlets

A Historical Sketch of the Wilmington Library, and Young Men's Association, with the Constitution, By-Laws, &c.,and a List of Officers & Members. Wilmington, Delaware: C. P. Johnson, Book & Job Printers, 1858.

An Explanation of the Modes of Establishing Free Libraries in Delaware with A Full Text of the State Library Laws and The Story of the Making of A Delaware Library. Dover, Delaware: The State Library Commission, 1915.

Exercises at the Opening of the New Building of The Wilmington Institute Free Library. Wilmington, Delaware, May Fifth, 1923.

Jones, Frank Morton. *Library Service for "Greater Wilmington", A report on the present service and future expansion of the Wilmington Institute Free Library.* The Wilmington Institute Free Library, 1926.

Miller, Thomas E. *The Wilmington Library: Institute of the Colonies.* Wilmington, Delaware: The Board of Managers, Wilmington Institute Library, 1976.

Nields, John P. *The Wilmington Public Library and The New Castle County Free Library: A Historical Sketch.* Wilmington, Delaware: The Wilmington Institute, 1943.

Opening Ceremony of the Wilmington Institute Library. Wilmington, Delaware, September, 1974.

Manuscripts

Bush, Charles W. "Wilmington Institute Officers, Directors and Managers, 1861-1943." Typescript, 1943.

Height, Esther L. "Survey Report, The Wilmington Institute Free Library with emphasis on The Children's Room." Submitted in partial fulfilment of the requirements for the degree of Master of Science in the School of Library Service, Columbia University. August, 1952.

Library, Reports, Blueprints, etc., 1917-1920, file #6871. Hagley Museum and Library.

Library, Sale of Property, 1919, file #6872. Hagley Museum and Library.

McKinstry, Linda Bove. "Delaware learned Societies: 1785-1893." Submitted in partial fulfilment of the requirements of the Master of Arts Degree. University of Delaware, June 1985.

"Minute Book of Wilmington Library Company from 1787 to 1818." Wilmington Library.

"Minutes of the Wilmington Institute, 1862-1866." Wilmington Library.

"Minutes of the Wilmington Institute, 1866-1873." Wilmington Library.

Wilmington Institute Free Library, 1915-1948, file #687. Pierre S. duPont Collection. Hagley Museum and Library.

Wilmington Institute Free Library, 1906-1915, file #2479. John J. Raskob Collection. Hagley Museum and Library.

"Proceedings of the Young Men's Association and the Executive Committee Thereof, Commencing 1855," Wilmington Library.

Reports

Annual Reports of the Wilmington Library, retained at the Wilmington Library.

1876, 1878, 1898-1899, 1899-1900, 1900-1901, 1917-1918, 1918-1919, 1921-1922, 1922-1923, 1923-1924, 1924-1925, 1927-1928, 1928-1929, 1929-1930, 1930-1931, 1931-1932, 1932-1933, 1933-1934, 1934-1935, 1935-1936, 1936-1937, 1937-1938, 1938-1939, 1939-1940, 1940-1941, 1941-1942, 1942-1943, 1943-1944, 1944-1945, 1945-1946, 1946-1947, 1947-1948, 1948-1949, 1949-1950, 1950-1951, 1951-1952, 1952-1953, 1953-1954, 1954-1955, 1955-1956, 1956-1957, 1957-1958, 1958-1959, 1959-1960, 1960-1961, 1961-1962, 1962-1963, 1963-1964, 1964-1965, 1965-1966, 1966-1967, 1967-1968, 1969-1970, 1970-1971, 1971-1972, 1972-1973, 1975-1976, 1977-1978, 1978-1979, 1979-1980, 1980-1981, 1981-1982, 1982-1983, 1983-1984, 1984-1985, 1985-1986, 1986-1987

Annual Reports of the Wilmington Library, retained at the Historical Society of Delaware.

1861, 1862, 1863, 1864, 1865, 1866, 1867, 1868, 1869, 1870, 1871, 1872, 1873, 1874, 1875, 1877, 1879, 1880, 1881, 1882, 1883, 1884, 1885, 1887, 1888, 1889, 1890, 1891, 1892, 1894-1895, 1895-1896, 1896-1897, 1897-1898, 1901-1902, 1902-1903, 1903-1904, 1904-1905, 1905-1906, 1906-1907, 1907-1908, 1908-1909, 1909-1910, 1910-1911, 1911-1912, 1912-1913, 1913-1914, 1914-1915, 1915-1916, 1916-1917, 1919-1920, 1920-1921, 1925-1926, 1926-1927, 1968-1969

Interviews

Interviews with John A. Munroe, John Minto Dawson, Richard Abrams, Esq., Edith C. Frank, Barbara Benson, Carol Hoffecker, Grace Husted, April 1988.

Interviews with David Burdash, Freda Campbell, May 1988.

Chronology

1754 Evidence of a Wilmington library

1788 Library company founded and incorporated by the General Assembly

1849 Moved to Fourth Street Market house owned by Athenaeum Company

1859 Incorporated as the Wilmington Institute

1861 Occupied new building at 8th and Market Streets

1894 Became a free library

1897 Rockford Branch established

1898 Traveling libraries begun in New Castle County

1915 Brandywine Branch established

1923 Moved to new building on Rodney Square

1925 Woodlawn Branch established

1927 Smythe gift toward New Castle County Free Library

1959 Concord Pike Branch Library opened

1967 Kirkwood Highway Branch Library opened

1969 Extensive renovations to Rodney Square building

1975 New Castle County Library Department and federated system established

1979 La Biblioteca del Pueblo established

1988 200th anniversary of Wilmington Library

Librarians, Presidents, Directors, and Managers of the Wilmington Library

Librarians

Isaac Starr, Jr.	1788
Stephen Hayes	1789
Robert Coram	1789
John Webster	1790
Edward Hewes	1793
Nathan Bassett	1829-30
Jonas Pusey	1830-31
Joseph H. James	1836
Caleb Kimber	1837
Joseph Bringhurst	1844-54
Gustavus Taylor	1854
Emmeline Griffith	1854
Hennrietta W. Breese	1854-1868
Augustus Wilmans	1868
Mary Resag, acting	1893-1894
Arthur W. Tyler	1894-1895
Willis F. Sewall	1895-1899
Enos Doan	1899-1900
George F. Bowerman	1901-1904
Irene D. Hillegas, act.	August-October 1904
Arthur L. Bailey	1904-1940
Emma L. Eckman, acting	February-August 1940
Harland A. Carpenter	1940-1964
Christopher B. Devan	1964-1970
Jack W. Bryant	1970-1975
David H. Burdash	1975-present

(Librarians are seldom mentioned by name in the early minutes. It is assumed that the librarian served until another one was named.)

Directors of the
Wilmington Library Company
1788-1857

John A. Allderdice	1846-51
Henry L. Alrich	1844
Jacob Alrichs	1829-31, 1833-43
Henry F. Askew	1834-37, 1844-46
W. W. Baker	1835-36
Richard H. Bayard	1832
Benjamin Betts	1847, 1852
William H. Billany	1857
Edward Bringhurst	1832, 1834-1845
James Bringhurst	1844, 1848
Joseph Bringhurst	1828-30
John Bullock	1828-31, 1833-34, 1837-40
George W. Bush	1847, 1855-57
L. P. Bush	1839-43, 1853
Jacob H. Byrnes	1846
Charles Canby	1841, 1844-57
William Canby	1857
Robert Carswell	1846-47
William Chandler	1831
Joseph W. Day	1857
William D. Dowe	1857
John Ferris	1835-36, 1838-39, 1841-44
Samuel Floyd, Jr.	1846-51
Thomas Garrett	1831-39
Allen Gawthorp	1857
Henry Gibbons	1832-36
Joseph Gilpin	1831-33
Dr. A. H. Grimshaw	1850-57
Willard Hall	1828-57
Caleb Harland	1849-52
Hanson Harman	1855-57
John Harris	1837
Milton Hartley	1846-48
Henry Heald	1828-29
John Hedges	1845-49
Samuel Hilles	1828-30
William S. Hilles	1850-51, 1856-57
Charles W. Howland	1857
Isaac Jackson	1830, 1833-34
George Jones	1837-41
Alexander Kelley	1857
Joseph Lee	1831
Samuel McCaully	1838

136

William McCaulley	1832
Robert McDonnell	1842-45
John McLear	1832
Aaron P. Osmond	1853-57
J. Morton Poole	1852-54
Jonas Pusey	1835-45, 1848-49
Joshua Pusey	1857
William Pyle	1848-52, 1854, 1857
John Reynolds	1828-34
George Reynolds	1841-45
Samuel Smith	1833
Albert Smith	1844
Charles Stewart	1853-57
William R. Stratton	1848-51
T. Clarkson Taylor	1853-57
William Travis	1854-55
J. F. Vaughan	1828-31
Jonas Wales	1828
Henry Warner	1840, 1843
E. A. Wilson	1845
Thomas Young	1842

Presidents of the
Wilmington Library Company
and the Wilmington Institute

Willard Hall	1830-37, 1842-57
Joshua T. Heald	1857-1859
William Canby	1860
Samuel Biddle	1861
William S. Hilles	1862
George W. Bush	1863
Dr. William R. Bullock	1864
Dr. J. F. Vaughan	1865
John H. Adams	1866
John P. McLear	1867
S. M. Harrington	1868
Daniel W. Taylor	1869
William H. Swift	1870
Anthony Higgins	1871
William M. Canby	1872
George H. Bates	1873
Mahlon M. Child	1874
Rev. T. Gardner Littell	1875
Howard M. Jenkins	1876

William S. Auchincloss	1877
John C. Cole	1878
Samuel A. Macallister	1879
Henry C. Conrad	1880
Frederic H. Robinson	1881
David W. Harlan	1882
Stansbury J. Willey	1883
George A. Elliott	1884
T. Allen Hilles	1885
Dr. Charles R. Jefferis	1886
Dr. John M. Curtis	1887
Isaac T. Johnson	1888
Thomas K. Porter	1889
Walter D. Bush	1890
Charles W. Pusey	1891
Lindley C. Kent	1892
Vincent G. Hazard	1893
William P. Taylor	1894
(Re-elected)	

Presidents of
The Wilmington Free Institute

William P. Taylor	1894-1910
Vincent G. Hazard	1910-1921
Hon. John P. Nields	1921-1943
Charles W. Bush	1943-1959
George Winchester	1959-1972
Edward B. du Pont	1972-1981
Willard A. Speakman, III	1981-present

138

Directors of the Wilmington Library and Young Men's Association Renamed the Wilmington Institute 1859-1893

John H. Adams	1860, 1862-66
W. H. Allderdice	1860
W. S. Auchincloss	1873-77
George H. Bates	1870-83
Nathaniel R. Benson, Jr.	1861-66
Samuel Biddle	1859-62
William H. Billany	1857-59
W. W. Birdsall	1885
Edward G. Bradford, Jr.	1873-79
James Bradford	1859-63
Ferris Bringhurst	1859
William Bringhurst	1862-63
Dr. William R. Bullock	1859-60, 1863-81
George W. Bush	1857-62
Henry Bush	1883-86
Walter D. Bush	1887-93 (new Board 1893-1905)
William Canby	1859-80
William M. Canby	1867-76
George S. Capelle	1860-62
Mahlon M. Child	1867-83
Mark M. Cleaver	1880-92
John C. Cole	1863-64 and 1869-77
Leighton Coleman	1864-66
Henry C. Conrad	1875-80
William T. Croasdale	1867-68
Dr. John M. Curtis	1882-90
William D. Dowe	1863-65
Henry C. Downward	1887-88
George A. Elliott	1878-93
J. Cloud Elliott	1863-66
H. F. Finnegan	1860-61
Henry Gawthrop	1861
Ignatius C. Grubb	1869, 1871-75
David W. Harlan	1877-85
Hanson Harman	1859
Samuel M. Harrington	1863-70
Holstein Harvey	1882-83
Vincent G. Hazard	1889-93 (new Board 1893-1921)
Pusey Heald	1859, 1862
Anthony Higgins	1865-72
T. Allen Hilles	1881-89

William S. Hilles	1859-64
Charles W. Howland	1859-73, 1886-89
Ellwood C. Jackson	1893 (new Board 1893-1919)
Howard M. Jenkins	1869-78
Dr. Charles R. Jefferis	1882-85, 1887-98
Isaac T. Johnson	1885-93 (new Board 1893-98)
Lindley C. Kent	1889-93 (new Board 1893-1916)
Thomas J. Lawson	1884-93
Rev. T. Gardner Littell	1867-83
Charles B. Lore	1861-64
Samuel A. Macallister	1870-81
Dr. David W. Maull	1866-68
J. Augustus McCaulley	1891-92
Morris McDowell	1863
John P. McLear	1857-59, 1866
J. Robinson Moore	1884-85
Dr. Samuel W. Murphy	1880-81
Benjamin Nields	1867-73
Wilmer Palmer	1890-93 (new Board 1893-1913)
Charles G. Phillips	1887-89
Thomas K. Porter	1884-93
Charles W. Pusey	1886-93 (new Board 1893-95)
Joseph Pyle	1861-62
William A. Reynolds	1868-72
Joseph A. Richardson	1872-93 (new Board 1893-96)
Frederic H. Robinson	1878-84 (new Board 1911-16)
Robert Emmitt Robinson	1860-62
Rev. C. D. Shaw	1871
P. T. E. Smith	1867-68
Samuel D. Smith	1874-78
Samuel K. Smith	1890-92
Clement B. Smyth	1861-66
William C. Spruance	1871-72
John W. Stapler	1865-66
William H. Swift	1864-70
Edward Tatnall, Jr.	1867-69, 1873-77
Henry L. Tatnall	1864-65
William Tatnall	1859-62
Daniel W. Taylor	1865-70, 1879-93
Edward T. Taylor	1857-59
T. Clarkson Taylor	1862
William P. Taylor	1890-92 (new Board 1893-1911)
Dr. J. Franklin Vaughan	1862-66
Dr. John P. Wales	1866-68
Leonard E. Wales	1859-62
Joseph R. Walter	1876-81
Stansbury J. Willey	1879-93
Daniel Woodall	1873-74
James Wooley	1860
Abram R. Woolston	1863

Managers of the Wilmington Institute
1893-1943

William P. Bancroft	1893-1911
George P. Bissell	1929-51*
H. Fletcher Brown	1931-43
C. Lalor Burdick	1941-44*
Philip Burnet	1917-28
Charles W. Bush	1923-62*
Henry T. Bush	1915-43
Lewis P. Bush	1905-14
Walter D. Bush	1893-1905 (old Board 1887-93)
William Michael Byrne	1896-1901
Lammot du Pont Copeland	1936-73*
Enos L. Doan	1893-96, 1898-99
H. Belin du Pont	1928-64*
Pierre S. du Pont	1918-28
Burton P. Fowler	1927-42
Leroy Harvey	1917-28
Vincent G. Hazard	1893-1921 (old Board 1889-93)
Rev. Cicero A. Henderson	1910-13
Edgar M. Hoopes, Jr.	1914-31
Ellwood C. Jackson	1893-1919 (old Board 1893)
Isaac T. Johnson	1893-1898 (old Board 1885-93)
Frank Morton Jones	1922-51*
Lindley C. Kent	1893-1916 (old Board 1889-93)
Rev. William Frederick Dickens Lewis	1899-1909
George B. Miller	1919-36
John Percy Nields	1895-1943
Herschel A. Norris	1901-23
Wilmer Palmer	1893-1913 (old Board 1890-93)
Charles W. Pusey	1893-95 (old Board 1886-93)
Joshua L. Pusey	1859
J. Edgar Rhoads	1916-74*
Frederic H. Robinson	1911-16 (old Board 1878-84)
William P. Taylor	1893-1911 (old Board 1890-92)
William P. White	1911-14

*Served beyond 1943

141

The Wilmington Library
Board of Managers
1943 to the Present

Richard J. Abrams	1971-present
Anita V. Biondi	1985-present
Alfred E. Bissell	1951-71
George P. Bissell	1943-51 (old Board 1927-43)
Elmer K. Bolton	1944-66
C. Lalor Burdick	1943-44 (old Board 1941-43)
Charles W. Bush	1943-62 (old Board 1923-43)
Henry M. Canby	1962-71
Lammot du Pont Copeland	1943-73 (old Board 1936-43)
John M. Dawson	1982
Brian J. Donnelly	1985
Edward B. du Pont	1964-present
Henry B. du Pont	1943-64 (old Board 1928-43)
Hon. Daniel L. Herrmann	1966-73
Michael L. Hershey	1977-present
Carol E. Hoffecker	1974-79
Joseph F. Hulihan	1987-present
Frank Morton Jones	1943-51 (old Board 1922-43)
George V. Kirk	1980-85
Antonia B. Laird	1974-78
Isabella Patty	1978-84
George Burton Pearson, Jr.	1943-77
Charles L. Reese, Jr.	1962-78
J. Edgar Rhoads	1943-74 (old Board 1922-43)
Arthur H. Richardson	1979-88
Clarence A. Southerland	1951-66
Willard A. Speakman III	1967-present
Richard L. Sutton	1974-present
Rodman Ward	1944-62
Eldridge J. Waters	1971-74
George Winchester	1943-73
William C. Wyer	1986-present

142

Index

Burdash, David, viii, x, 135
Burdick, C. Lalor, 141, 142
Burnet, Philip, 141
Bush, Charles W., 138, 141, 142
Bush, George W., 27, 136, 137, 139
Bush, Henry T., 139, 141
Bush, Lewis P., 136, 141
Bush, Walter D., 138, 139, 141
Bushman, Claudia L., viii, ix, x
Business and Technical library, (Science, Technology and Business
    Department), 93, 94, 100, 112
Butler, Kezia, 21
Byrne, William Michael, 141
Byrnes, Jacob H., 136
Byrnes, Samuel, 14
Camp Meade, Maryland, 67
Campbell, Freda, viii
Canby, Charles, 136
Canby, Henry, M., 142
Canby, William, 136, 137, 139
Canby, William M., 137, 139
Capelle, George S., 139
Capelle, Joseph, 14
Caritat's Circulating Library, 21
Carnegie, Andrew, 45-46, 48, 61
Carpenter, Harland A., 86, 91, 135
Carpenter, Sarah J., 33
Carpenters' Hall, 7
Carswell, Robert, 136
Catholic Cemeteries of the Diocese of Wilmington, 97
Chandler, William, 136
Charitable Library of Concord, Massachusetts, 22
Child, Mahlon M., 137, 139
Children's services, 52, 94, 101, 109, 116
Christiana, Delaware, 79
Circulating libraries: England 20, United States, 20, 22
City of Wilmington, 4, 11, 35, 98, 99, 104; bond issue, 68; council,
    6, 50; library support, 63, 79
Civil War, 34
Clark, John, 14
Cleaver, Mark M., 139
Cole, John C., 138, 139
Coleman, Leighton, 139
Colored Settlement, 56; "library for colored people," 83
Computers, 112-113
Concord Pike Branch, 97, 106
Connecticut, 8
Conrad, Henry C., 138, 139
Constitution, United States, vii, 3

Cook, Lynda, viii
Cooper, Dr. Constance, viii
Copeland, Lammot du Pont, 141, 142
Coram, Robert, 14, 15, 135
Corbitt, William, 14
Corner Ketch, Delaware, 79
Court House Square, 62
Craig, Frederick, 13, 14
Croasdale, William T., 139
Curtis, Dr. John M., 138, 139
Davenport Boys, 33-34
Dawson, John M., 142
Day, Joseph W., 136
Debating Society, 25
Defoe, Daniel, 21
Delaplain, James, 14
Delaware Academy of Natural Sciences, 25
Delaware Army National Guard, 99
Delaware City, Delaware, 78
Delaware Heritage Commission, vii
Delaware Philosophical Society, 18, 19
Delaware Rapid Inter Library Loan, 111
Delaware River, 18
Delawareana, 54, 73-74
Devan, Christopher B., 100, 135
Devine, Donn, viii
Diamond State Guards, 33
Dickinson, John, vii, 13, 16, 21, 29, 30
Dickinson, Anna, 32
Doan, Enos L., 135, 141
Donnelly, Brian J., 142
Douglass, Frederick, 32
Dowe, William D., 136,139
Downward, Henry C., 139
Drexel University, 113
du Pont, Edward B., 138, 142
du Pont, Henry B., 141, 142
du Pont, Pierre S., 63, 64, 67, 68, 69, 141
Duplicate Pay Collection, 55
DuPont building, 62, 117
DuPont Company, 62
DuPont Engineering Company, 68
Eckman, Emma L., 135
Elgin Marbles, 71
Elliott, George A., 138, 139
Elliott, J. Cloud, 139
England, 7
Enlightenment, 6
Erie Canal, 21

Evans, Oliver, 21
Everett, Edward, 32
Excelsior Brass Band, 33
Federal Building, 62
Ferris, D. Benjamin, 4, 7
Ferris, John, 11, 14, 136
Films, 113
Finnegan, H. F., 139
First Presbyterian Church, 62, 64
Fitzgerald, Ellenor, 21
Floyd, Samuel, Jr., 136
Folsom, Henry, 104
Fourth Street Market House, 16, 25, 30
Fowler, Burton P., 141
Frank, Edith, 86
Frank, William P., viii, 95
Franklin, Benjamin, 7, 22
Franklin Lyceum, 25
Friends of the Library, 115
Frisby, Sarah, 14, 15
Garrett, Thomas, 136
Garrison, Dr. Guy, 113
Gates Wide Open, 32
Gawthorp, Allen, 136
Gawthrop, Henry, 139
General Assembly, i, 14, 116
Gibbons, Henry, 136
Gilles, Mrs. John P., 30
Gilpin, Joseph, 136
Gilpin, Major R. P., 34
Githens, Alfred M., 66, 68-73, 85
Glee Club, 30
Goldey's Commercial College, 64
Goldsmith, Oliver, 21
Govatos, John, 63
Grand Opera House, 39
Great Books discussions, 91, 92
Great Depression, 86
Greeley, Horace, 32
Griffith, Emmeline, 135
Grimshaw, Col. A. H., 36, 136
Grubb, Ignatius C., 139
Hagley Community House, 56
Hall, Willard, 136, 137
Harlan, David W., 138, 139
Harland, Caleb, 136
Harman, Hanson, 136, 139
Harrington, Samuel M., 137, 139
Harris, John, 136

Jones, Dr. Frank Morton, 84-86, 141, 142
Jones, George, 136
Jos. Bancroft & Sons Co., 51, 81-82
Junto, 7
Juvenile Literary Society, 25
Kelley, Alexander, 136
Kelley, James, 62
Kennedy, President John F., 99
Kent, Lindley C., 138, 140, 141
Kimber, Caleb, 135
King, Dr. Martin Luther King, Jr., 99
Kirk, George V., 142
Kirkwood Highway Branch, 78, 97, 98, 106
Kresge store, 64
La Biblioteca del Pueblo, 114-115
Ladies' Aid Society of Grace Church, 33
Ladies' Association for the Relief of Sick & Wounded Soldiers, 34
Ladies Library, 21
Laird, Antonia B., 142
Lammott, Capt. Robert, 34
Lawson, Thomas J., 140
Lea, James, Jr., 11
Lea, Thomas, 11, 14
Lee, Joseph, 136
Letters on the Female Mind, 21
Levy Court of New Castle County, 97
Lewis, the Rev. William Frederick Dickens, 141
Libraries: athenaeum, 8; free, 45; history, 3; proprietary, 7;
        history, vii
Library Association, 6
Library Commission of the State of Delaware, 98, 104
Library Company of Philadelphia, 7, 8, 11, 22
Library Company of Wilmington, 11; articles of association, 12;
        book list, 21; charter, 13; collection, 22; constitution, 16;
        directors, 15; growth, 16; librarian, 13; merger, 26;
        minutes, 14; move, 25; opened doors, 13; seal, 13;
        solicit members, 15; stock certificate, 18; subscription, 20.
        See also Wilmington Library
Library Services and Construction Act, 97
Life of Jefferson Davis, 32
Lincoln, Abraham, 35
Lincoln collection, 74
Literacy Volunteers of America, 115-116
Littell, the Rev. T. Gardner, 137, 140
Longfellow, Henry Wadsworth, 52
Longwood Foundation, 97, 98
Lore, Charles B., 140
Lyceum, 19, 20
Macallister, Samuel A., 138, 140

Maine, 45
Martin, John, 14
Masonic Temple, 39
Massachusetts, 45, 47
Mather, Mary H. Askew, 78
Maull, Dr. David W., 140
May, Thomas, 13
McCaulley, J. Augustus, 140
McCaulley, William, 137
McCaully, Samuel, 136
McComb-Winchester mansion, 62
McDonnell, Robert, 137
McDowell, Morris, 140
McKinly, John, 14
McLear, John P., 137, 140
McLoud, John P., 27
McNinch, Marjorie, viii
Mechanics' libraries, 27-29
Medical Society of Delaware, 19, 20, 33
Methuen, Massachusetts, 53
Microfiche reader, 101
Microfilm, 92, 93
Miller, George B., 141
Milton, John, 21
Minquadale Home, 85
Mobile service, 77-78, 99
Moll Flanders, 32
Montague, Mary Wortly, 21
Moore, J. Robinson, 140
Morton, Nellie, 79
Mosley and His Men, 32
Munroe, Dr. John A., viii
Murdock, Patrick, 11, 14
Murphy, Dr. Samuel W., 140
Music programs, 92
National Library Week, 105
New Castle County, 103-104
New Castle County Council, 104
New Castle County Levy Court, 79
New Castle County Library, 77, 79, 96; branches, 53; building
    announced, 97; consolidation, 111; established, 106;
    funding, 92; library study, 113
New Castle Library Company, 15
New England, 20, 22
New Hampshire, 45, 47
New York City, 21, 47
Nicola, Lewis, 21
Nields, Benjamin, 140
Nields, John Percy, 64, 66-70, 74, 91, 138, 141

Night School Association, 38
Norris, Herschel A., 141
Northeast Partners, 103
Novels, 21
Observation on Novel Reading, 21
Odd Fellows Building, 100
Ogletown, Delaware, 79
Olivet Presbyterian Church, 56
Osmond, Aaron P., 137
Palmer, Wilmer, 140, 141
Parthenon, 71
Paschall, Henry, 14
Patty, Isabella, 142
Peabody, George, 28
Pearson, George Burton, Jr., 142
People's Settlement, 56
Peterborough, New Hampshire, 46-47
Peterson, Ellen, viii
Philadelphia, Pennsylvania, 7, 18, 21
Phillips, Charles G., 140
Phillips, Wendell, 32
Phonograph records, 92, 101
Planet Mills Manufacturing, 56
Polish station, 56
Poole, J. Morton, 137
Poole, William, 11, 14
Pope, Alexander, 21
Port Penn, Delaware, 78
Porter, Thomas K., 138, 140
Priestly, Joseph, 21
Public Building, 62
Pusey, Charles W., 138, 140, 141
Pusey, Jonas, 135, 137
Pusey, Joshua, 137, 141
Pyle, Joseph, 140
Pyle, William, 137
Quakers, 3; merchants, 18; thought, 21
Read Aloud Delaware, 116
Reese, Charles L., 101, 142
Renzulli, William F, 112
Resag, Mary, 135
Revolutionary War, 6, 20, 21
Reynolds, George, 137
Reynolds, Henry, 14
Reynolds, John, 137
Reynolds, William A., 140
Rhoads, J. Edgar, 141, 142
Richardson, Arthur H., 142
Richardson, Joseph A., 140